Learning from Our Lives

Learning from Our Lives

Using Educational Biographies with Adults

Pierre Dominicé

Foreword by Alan B. Knox

JOSSEY-BASS
A Wiley Company
San Francisco

Jossey-Bass books and products are available through most bookstores.
To contact Jossey-Bass directly, call (888) 378-2537, fax to
(800) 605-2665, or visit our website at www.josseybass.com.

Substantial discounts on bulk quantities of Jossey-Bass books are
available to corporations, professional associations, and other
organizations. For details and discount information, contact the
special sales department at Jossey-Bass.

Library of Congress Cataloging-in-Publication Data

Dominicé, Pierre.
   Learning from our lives : using educational biographies with adults /
Pierre Dominice ; foreword by Alan Knox. — 1st ed.
       p.   cm. — (The Jossey-Bass higher and adult education series)
Includes bibliographical references and index.
   ISBN 0-7879-1031-7 (hardcover : alk. paper)
   1. Education—Biographical methods. 2. Adult education.   3. Adult
learning.   I. Title.   II. Series.
   LB1029.B55   D64   2000
   374.139—dc21

FIRST EDITION
HB Printing   10 9 8 7 6 5 4 3 2 1

The Jossey-Bass

Higher and Adult Education Series

Contents

Foreword

The recent burgeoning interest of North American educators in asking students to write and share life story narratives has been fostered by an aging population, women's studies, and a growing appreciation of the importance of critical reflection on indigenous—that is, local—knowledge. In addition, a major influence has been the earlier and more widespread attention given to educational biography by European educators. Pierre Dominicé has been at the forefront of this pioneering approach to adult learning, which emphasizes the developmental process and subjective meanings. Although similar to life story writing and the recording of oral history, the preparation of educational biographies enables adults to reflect on and discuss their own learning experiences. The result is enhanced critical thinking, an active search for meaning, collaborative interpretation, and attention to situational influences.

Practitioners throughout the helping professions are beginning to facilitate the preparation of educational biographies. Consider these examples:

- Educators help returning students prepare educational biographies that illuminate themes in the students' motives, satisfactions, frustrations, and strategies for success.

- Career counselors use insights from depth psychology to encourage adults to write educational biographies that may help them consider their gifts and abilities.

- Librarians help patrons share memories through narratives, and in this process young adults attend to their search for identity and self-confidence and to their changing interpersonal relations and older adults engage in life review. In both instances learning is a major theme.

- Educators serve as mentors to adult students, enabling these learners to use insights from their educational biographies to assess new opportunities, make flexible use of their knowledge in new ways, and engage in life planning.

- Human resource development specialists enable business and industry staff to share stories in a personal, immediate, and dynamic way to promote empathic understanding of others, build community, and help others facing similar situations.

- Environmentalists invite adults interested in environmental issues to write educational biographies that help them recognize how they learned to care about the environment, share their stories, and deepen their understanding and commitment.

- Religious educators videotape the oral histories of congregation members as they recall their spiritual journeys.

- Teachers invite elders into the classroom to share their first-hand stories and then participate in intergenerational discussion.

- Educators help professionals in continuing education learn how to learn more effectively by reflecting on the processes and results of their past learning efforts and by building on insights related to professional, societal, personal, and situational influences, encouraging interactions that can contribute to improved practice.

- Retirement and elder care staff arrange for older adults to write about their reminiscences and to discuss these experiences among themselves and share them with families and caregivers.

In this book Professor Dominicé provides the rationale and examples that can encourage helping professionals to initiate and strengthen their use of educational biography, whether they are working in formal educational programs or in informal and largely self-directed learning activities. Preparing and sharing educational biographies can help adults reflect on what they know and on how individuals extract meaning from experience. By reflecting on authentic learning experiences, adults can come to appreciate their indigenous knowledge. As participants in learning situations, they can become more willing to assume responsibility for guiding their own learning activities as they gain confidence that they have sufficient background to do so.

As the educational biography approach is increasingly used to help adults learn, North American innovations can enrich the activities pioneered by Professor Dominicé and his European colleagues, thus enhancing and continuing this transatlantic exchange.

University of Wisconsin-Madison   Alan B. Knox

Preface

Educational biography is an adult education approach that emphasizes the subjective meanings and the developmental process of
adult learning. In this approach, adult learners prepare and share life
histories that become vehicles through which these learners can
reflect on their educational experiences. Through oral and written
narratives, educational biography offers the values of reminiscence
and the interpretation of experience and influences upon that experience. It is a distinctive approach to teaching and learning because
its main purpose is to help adults deepen their understanding of
their own ways of learning and of their existing knowledge. It is a
narrative research method that helps people identify their learning
processes in adulthood.

Many people think of their learning in terms of their formal
education, especially their schooling when they were young. Educational biography activities can reveal such formal learning experiences in all their complexity, illuminating influences, learning
styles, benefits, and dissatisfactions. However, learning is also always ongoing in all aspects of adult life, through the vehicles of
informal education and experiential learning. Educational biography can help adults appreciate the pervasiveness of their total
learning, reflect on and interpret their experience, and gain insight
into their singular learning processes.

Educational biography makes adult learners partners in an inquiry process. It involves adults in a collaborative inquiry, a partnership akin to action research that deepens their understanding of
the process and impact of learning activities. Educational biography

can also promote self-actualization, especially when the individual recognizes his or her own transformational learning arising out of major change events in family, work, and community. Inquiry into these normal developmental transitions produces a heightened readiness to learn.

Educational biography is neither an instrument for collecting data nor a new model for teaching. Instead it offers a way for an adult education practitioner to incorporate a modest and often exploratory inquiry project into an educational program for adults. Each of the many and varied types of educational programs and activities for adults can encourage participants to prepare some form of educational biography in order to learn why and how to learn. This emphasis on learning can complement the more organized forms of instruction common to adult education. Conducted in accord with a democratic, humanist vision of society, an educational biography approach can guide adults' inquiry into the many influences on and results from their learning experiences, helping them understand how these influences and results relate to the complexities of their lives. Educators can facilitate this inquiry process so that participants also recognize and explore the societal context of learning and education and the interdependence between that context and learning. Education, first of all, should be analyzed from within. That is, the process of adult learning should be studied as it evolves and through its own dynamics. Research on adult learning should take account of the situations in which that learning takes place. Such research should recognize that adults have their own understanding of the ways they learn, their styles and their difficulties. Moreover, adults interpret relevant data wherever these data come from.

Purpose

Learning from Our Lives provides a detailed exploration of the reasons for, a *rationale* for, using educational biography approaches in adult education. It also presents examples that illustrate various uses of these life history activities and that focus on learning in a number of settings. This combination of rationale and examples is intended to assist adult educators in adapting the basic concepts of the approach to their own goals and highly varied situations. Moreover, preparing and sharing educational biographies can benefit adult educators as well as the students with whom they work.

Life history reflection can foster the dialectic between the personal and social aspects of learning. The rationale for educational biography pays attention to both learner empowerment through the inquiry process (an instance of the personal) and learner collaboration with educators and peers to produce, share, and interpret educational biographies (an instance of the situational).

Perspective

Scholars from various countries, including the United States, are becoming increasingly interested in the use of educational biography. This rationale for the use of educational biography reflects a European perspective and Europeans' early interest in educational biography. One of the first and largest research networks of the European Society for Research in the Education of Adults has taken as its focus life history and the biographical approach. More than one hundred adult education researchers from all parts of Europe have participated in the international research conferences "Life History and Biography in Adult Education" held in Geneva (1993, 1995, and 1997), Vienna (1994), and Rome (1996).

In addition to the perspective shaped by international, and especially European, exchange on this topic, I have a personal perspective. This book was written in Europe by a French-speaking European from Switzerland. In it I attempt to introduce concepts about adult learning into contexts beyond the European contexts in which they were conceived. I raise questions about international cooperation and societal context. On an even more personal level, I am the father of three bilingual children raised in a Euro-American family, so I have experienced cultural similarities and differences up close and personal. Life is a learning process.

My overall perspective on educational biography reflects some fundamental viewpoints. Given the various settings and programs in which educational biography can be used, I have emphasized understanding ways of knowing more than acquiring detailed methods and techniques for guiding the process. I have also sought to express profound respect for the uniqueness of each person and his or her distinctive life history. A single life history can be uniquely meaningful for author and reader even though its meaning borrows from a cultural heritage built upon generations of biographies. Life is each person's singular version of an old story. We are quite different as human beings in our varied cultural contexts, but the solutions we find for the main conflicts of our lives have similarities. Even that which we consider original to an individual will have somewhere a cultural origin. As the French philosopher Paul Ricoeur (1986) has written: "The other person is another person similar to me, and a person like me. Like me, my contemporaries, my predecessors, and my successors can say 'I.' It is in this way that I am historically connected with all others" (p. 227; my translation).

Inviting adults to examine their previous learning experiences can empower them to assume greater responsibility for their current and future learning in any setting. I have come to appreciate the importance of life events and contexts as they contribute to the personal and sociocultural complexity of a person's life. Educational biography emphasizes the learner's viewpoint, revealing how the adult uses experiential learning to educate himself or herself. The resulting insights can help adult educators focus on learning and not just teaching.

Educational biography is a means to understand adult learning more broadly and deeply. It complements more formal adult education programs that emphasize instruction related to organized content. Even a comprehensive curriculum does not guarantee that the desired adult proficiency will result from a program. Socialization and personal identity remain key factors in the process of adult learning.

My exploration of educational biography emerged from my interest in the evaluation of both the process and outcomes of adult education. In spite of much research and evaluation the adult learning process still needs much clarification. We still know very little about influences such as cultural or family backgrounds, early schooling, work experience, and teaching approaches on adults' efforts to enhance their proficiencies. The life history approach I present in this book is an attempt to deal with the many-sided dynamics of adult learning.

Early on in my work with educational biography I analyzed one hundred educational biographies. Many of the themes, procedures, and rationales discussed in this book emerged from this analysis. A central insight was that recognition of indigenous, or local, knowledge is central to both greater self-directedness on the part of learners and responsive guidance on the part of educators. Appreciation of this finding can help educators avoid depersonalizing their adult students as a result of overgeneralizing about them.

Audience

The main audience for this book consists of the practitioners who plan and conduct all types of educational programs for adults, in schools, universities, corporations, nonprofit organizations, community agencies, and other settings. The rationale for educational biography presented here suggests how practitioners can collaborate with adult learners to explore life history themes relating to personal and social learning, enabling learners to become increasingly self-directed in their learning activities.

Helping adults gain insights into their learning can empower them. Helping those who help adults learn understand why educational biography works can empower these educators to guide adults' efforts to explore their educational biographies. Because most people who help adults learn do so as volunteers or part-time staff, they are likely to require assistance from the practitioners who provide program coordination and leadership if they are to discover and use an educational biography approach. Thus teachers of practitioners will also benefit from this book. Moreover, when program coordinators undertaking graduate study in adult and continuing education are exposed to educational biography as students, it can have a multiplier effect in the field of practice.

Overview of the Contents

Chapter One provides an introduction to and overview of educational biography. The main ideas include educational biography's focus on empowering adult learners by helping them analyze their own experience with learning and education, situational influences, and life transitions, and ways to facilitate an educational biography approach.

Chapter Two describes in greater depth practitioners' experience with major educational biography approaches, including written and oral narratives, and with interpreting and sharing life history perspectives on learning and education. The chapter looks in particular at my own educational biography seminar at the University of Geneva.

Chapter Three presents a review of the literature, concentrating on various examples of more modest educational biography approaches that occur in particular contexts and address particular themes. It concludes with comments on their similarities and differences.

The succeeding chapters offer insights and examples from analysis of educational biographies. They also discuss the questions and procedures that educators can use to guide adults' preparation of educational biographies. Chapter Four explores how adults educate themselves in various settings, including family and school. A major theme is the way experiential learning helps people affirm themselves as learners, in contrast to the detachment that preparatory education students can feel.

The main theme of Chapter Five is adults' ways of thinking as men and women functioning in family, school, and workplace. Attention is also given to the influence of various subcultures.

Learners' needs and motivations constitute the focus of Chapter Six. Educational biographies reveal these needs and motivations and also adults' dreams as they relate to adult development and the transformation of our educational institutions.

In Chapter Seven the main theme is helping learners name, or put words to, their experiences and world. Interpretation can help adults recognize the nature and value of their experiential learning and indigenous knowledge. However, practitioners must also be prepared to help adults deal with important issues that emerge from this interpretation.

Educational biography can also help adult learners gain a new understanding of evaluation. This is the main theme of Chapter Eight, which addresses, among other topics, the power relationships that influence education and educational goals, the uses of evaluation conclusions, and formative evaluation as interpretation.

Chapter Nine concludes *Learning from Our Lives* with a discussion of creating conditions for successful adult learning based on the main themes raised by the educational biography approach. The major conclusions pertain to the ways adult educators using the educational biography approach can celebrate the diverse life histories of their adult learners and empower these adults to function more effectively in a changing world.

Acknowledgments

If this book is a European contribution to the U.S. debate on adult education, it is also a way to manifest my gratitude to a country that has on many different occasions been very hospitable to me. I have learned some of what I know in the United States, thanks to family, friends, and scholars who have shared with me the warmness of their convictions and the openness of their ideas. Jossey-Bass will always remain important to me as the very generous source of one opportunity to express myself in another cultural world. The invitation from Lynn Luckow to write a book was the first step of a long adventure that remained a challenge for years. I am also grateful to the many friends who have encouraged me. I wish to thank Jack Mezirow in particular, who kept telling me that this book had to be written. I have received great help with my English from two English-speaking teachers and editors who live in Geneva: Sally Beall and Dawn Bloss-Dimond. I thank them both warmly. I want to also express my deep gratitude to Elspeth MacHattie who did magnificent work as copyeditor. Last but not least, I am indebted to Alan B. Knox, who not only encouraged me constantly but rescued my project at the right time. Working with him, through many different means of communication, has been a great experience of friendship and international cooperation. Without his generosity and help this book could not have been finished, and he deserves my deepest thankfulness.

Geneva, Switzerland   Pierre F. Dominicé
March 2000

The Author

Pierre F. Dominicé is professor of adult education at the University of Geneva, Switzerland. He holds university degrees from the Sorbonne in Paris and the Union Theological Seminary in New York; he earned his doctoral degree in education at the University of Geneva.

He has directed several research projects financed by the Swiss National Fund for Scientific Research (FNRS) and is the author of studies in the field of evaluation and adult learning. His most recent previous book, written in French, dealt with educational biography.

Dominicé is president of the International Association for Life History Applied to Adult Education (ASIHVIF) and a member of the steering committee of the European Society for Research in the Education of Adults (ESREA).

Learning from Our Lives

Chapter One

Learning as an
Active Search for Meaning

In university, college, and corporate classrooms, in workshops and seminars in many settings, more and more adult students are preparing biographies, narratives examining both the formal and informal learning they have experienced so far in their lives. These adult learners may be professionals returning to the classroom to further their specialized knowledge, they may be individuals who have come to feel their earlier education was incomplete, or they may be adult educators or in training to become adult educators. The time allotted to preparing these biographies may be only two or three days, providing learners with an introduction to this approach to learning about one's own learning, or it may be a few academic year, requiring learners to commit to a much deeper interpretation of their experience. Every adult has experiences of learning that he or she can reflect on in an educational biography.

The expression *educational biography* was created early in my research, almost intuitively. I kept it after becoming more aware of the life history methodology. I like this expression because it points directly to the object of the research inquiry. A person's life history is understood as an educational process, and this biographical approach takes place in the context of higher education.

Different expressions have been used lately in the field of education: life cycle, autobiography, life narrative. Each term reveals a specific approach. But educational biography is not the same as autobiography. Writing an autobiography is an individual choice; the work belongs to the author from the beginning to the end. Authors of autobiographies may write about their life history from any perspective they wish. They might want to leave their close family a testimony of their past or they might wish to publish a book, talking about their lives to the public at large. The magnitude of the project does not matter. They have the power to do whatever they like, even to drop the project if it does not work out. A diary, a novel based on one's own life, a formal autobiography— there are many ways a person can present a part or the whole journey of his or her life. Some sociologists who have used life history as a methodology, such as Maurizio Catani, consider themselves public writers for a person unable to write his or her own autobiography. Catani's *Journal de Mohammed* (1973), the story of an Algerian immigrant in France, is an example of an autobiography coming out of collaborative work. As Catani says, it has a first and a second author, the sociologist being the second and the first being the real author, who was illiterate and could not write for himself.

In contrast, although adult learners are free to decide in the first place whether they want to attend sessions that focus on educational biography, they speak and write educational biographies only because these narratives have been requested by their teachers, and they do so within a structure. In the approach I have used, each learner is asked, and agrees, to present his or her biography in an oral and written version. Each learner belongs to a small group in which group members will interpret each other's educational biographies, and each learner also relates to the teacher. These learners sign a contract they have constructed with the group. Thus they have a different impetus from the autobiographer, and they have a different purpose. They are creating life histories but histories of a specific kind, focused on each author's learning, not simply any aspect of life that he or she chooses.

Basic Concepts

This chapter provides an overview of the basic concepts that underlie the use of educational biography in adult education: the characteristics of the adult learner that make educational biographies valuable, the web of life in which people move and are affected by transitions and social contexts, the individual empowerment arising from educational biography, the collaborative interpretation of learning and educational experiences that helps students reflect more deeply on those experiences, and the need for a multidisciplinary analysis of any necessarily subjective educational biography. These basic concepts not only constitute the rationale for asking adult learners to engage in educational biography but also point the way to successfully applying this process. They tell us not only why to practice this method of learning about learning but how to practice it successfully.

Extracts from three written narratives give the reader an initial look at real educational biographies and a better grasp of the potential insights such narratives offer to their authors and the others who help interpret them. The chapter then concludes with some observations about educational biography as an emerging trend.

Although this introductory chapter contains only a short view of the educational biography approach described in detail in subsequent chapters, it shows how each narrative results from a reflective attempt to collect various elements of a whole life history in order to help give life its meaning. Education is related to life events, experiences, and changes, and these give perspective to an educational biography. This perspective not only informs adult learners but offers them some basic data for thinking about education as a much broader phenomenon than formal learning alone.

The Adult Learner

Beatrice belongs to a category of adults who have been called *patchworkers* (Alheit, 1995). She has just turned twenty-nine years of age. She has explored different paths that often conflict. In her educational biography she relates that she holds "a certificate for providing children's security at school, a diploma in music, a high school degree in the sciences, a license for being a masseuse, half a degree in clinical psychology, a federal certificate for being a nursery-gardener, a diploma for conducting biodance, and a few more certificates." She worked in a circus as a cook for a while after dropping out of university, and she has traveled in several parts of the world. As she emphasizes: "My journey reflects a deep search for myself. . . . All my traveling here and abroad has been a quest for my cultural identity." Beatrice has learned by opening pathways leading her to a broader perspective. She builds projects "with an unending wish to find a balance between attractive sides of myself: body and mind, heaven and earth." She is lucid about herself and recognizes "being alone," "in my skin," "feeling what I feel." Looking over her life she refers to the capacity to decide and "to think for myself," as if the various explorations she went through had helped her to chose her own way of life.

The preparation of an educational biography can help adults better understand their own learning process. By confronting and reflecting on the learning moments in their own lives, they understand the extent to which learning in many different situations is an active search for meaning. As they think of themselves as the subject of their own biography, they are helped to accept that they hold their life in their hands even as they also recognize that their life's course and its related learning are subject to many influences. As adults gain a life history perspective on their learning, they typically clarify their concept of adulthood, recognize the centrality of interdependent social behavior to their lives, and appreciate that maturity continues to develop throughout adulthood.

Most adult learning occurs outside formal education. This experiential learning is commonly referred to as informal, or nonformal, education. It is akin to acculturation and socialization. This experiential base of learning has long been recognized. In addition, contemporary attention to experiential learning and indigenous, or local, knowledge gives us the constructivist perspectives on meaning formation, showing us how to view knowledge as tentative and socially constructed. This view places a premium on authentic learning experiences that entail reflecting on what is known and on how meaning is extracted from experience. Educational biography helps adults recognize how their previous experience and knowledge influence their new learning. As adult learners improve their critical thinking, they are better able to recognize assumptions and beliefs, make sense of the complexities of their lives, and understand major societal influences (Candy, 1991; Jackson and Caffarella, 1994; Merriam, 1993; Merriam and Brockett, 1997).

It can be empowering for adults to appreciate the increasing centrality of learning in today's complex and changing world. Moreover, reviewing their own histories of learning and education can help them become more self-directed learners. They become more willing to assume responsibility for guiding their own learning activities when they feel confident that they have sufficient background to do so (Candy, 1991; Pratt, 1988). In recent decades the long-standing writings of humanist psychology that emphasize self-actualization and learner-centered education have been supplemented by writings on self-directed learning and learning how to learn and on critical theory and perspective transformation. These writings buttress the rationale for educational biography by emphasizing the connection between individual learners and the societal contexts within which they function. These writings also support the value of guiding learners' efforts to understand such complex relationships at the personal level (Mezirow, 1991; Mezirow and Associates, 1990).

The Web of Life

Originating from a Third World country and living in Switzerland, Mary has chosen the images of a partitioned circle and a palimpsest to describe how the different facets of her life—a variety of places, cultures, training programs, and vocational experiences—all fit together: "By making out of my life a design looking like a wheel divided at the radius, I could look at my entire life. Finally, I have found all the pieces of the puzzle, and I was able to interpret this design. . . . I have found myself as a totality and I have recognized myself. . . . By making out of this raw material a palimpsest, I have seen that everything was there. I could read it over again, make connections and find their meaning. . . . In this palimpsest, I have found myself as one piece and no more divided, as I have felt often before. . . . I want to be myself. I want an identity that I decide to build instead of the plurality of my cultural experiences. I have taken the responsibility to compose, as we compose a cluster of flowers, with this diversity."

Life history narratives can reveal the ways in which living systems form a web of life. They can make it increasingly clear that the personal and societal aspects of life are connected. In addition, different adults have quite different modes of learning, and these modes are influenced by the ways individuals organize their lives. We each bring forth our world by living, because to live is to know, and what we know serves as a lens through which we interpret new experiences (Candy, 1991). We help to construct our own reality. Thus each biography has its own truth.

Educational biographies can help adult learners recognize social and interpersonal influences on their lives and educational activities. Preparing a life history focused on learning can also clarify the interdependence of biographical themes, major life transitions, and educational activities, calling learners' attention to both processes and outcomes in their lives and learning. A focus on specific occupational activities can result in a similar clarification (Schön, 1987). These narratives can also reveal formerly hidden influences, such as cultural traditions and beliefs.

Currently, the literature is giving increasing attention to the societal context that influences adult learning (Jarvis, 1987), that is, to an adult's current social, economic, and political environments and not just to his or her personal past. These societal influences are powerful. They are seen to set structural limits and offer opportunities that also contribute to an adult's unique subjective experience. Biographical learning helps adults discover influential dialectical, personal-systemic relationships such those among contingencies, needs, and resources. Local role changes in family, work, and community have been found to trigger a heightened readiness to learn. Concepts such as experiential learning and situational cognition are enabling adult educators to gain a more comprehensive under-standing of the authentic learning activities likely to produce trans-fer of knowledge and competency (Jackson and Caffarella, 1994). Such learning activities may focus on individual efforts to achieve personal change or on collective efforts to achieve social change (Freire, 1970; Mezirow, 1991).

Taking the societal aspects of a life into account adds to the complexity, paradoxes, and contradictions found in any educa-tional biography; nevertheless it is important to consider the soci-etal aspects of change in family, work, and community along with the personal aspects of life. Today such changes and the directions they may take are difficult to predict, so traditional solutions to change tend to be inadequate. Insights from their own educational biographies can prepare adults to assess new opportunities, to use knowledge flexibly and in new ways, and to guide their own life planning. Adult educators who have gained such insights from their own lives can serve as mentors to adult learners as they in turn learn from their biographies (Daloz, 1986).

Empowerment

Entering the university at forty years old had a deep biographical meaning for Marc. "How could I be myself with what others have given me, imposed upon me, have offered or refuse to offer? The beginning of my studies at the university at the age of forty has had for me the meaning that I have become the actor of my life—even though it is through psychotherapy that I have finally learned to say, 'I.' "

The preparation and use of educational biographies can em-power adult learners and the adult educators who facilitate the process. Collaboration between facilitators and adult learners is fundamental, whether learners are engaged in a class or workshop exclusively concerned with educational biography and including coaching and discussion among peers who exchange narratives or are taking part in less extensive educational biography approaches in conjunction with either formal education or self-directed learning. This collaboration is similar to the collaboration in action science and participatory research. The educator who facilitates the process helps students to focus their narratives on their adult learning but to pay some attention to their pre-adult learning as well. Many adults find that their school years have left them with painful memories. They hated some teachers and have felt unable to recover from receiving bad grades or failing to win a diploma. As one woman wrote in her narrative: "I cannot get over the fact that I failed at the end of high school. The image I have of myself is forever damaged." Educational biography gives adult learners an opportunity to deal with this past, put words to their anger, and share their feelings. As they interpret each other's narratives in groups and reflect on their school years, they might discover that in the past they learned more than they first thought. This analysis of experience works to create a kind of locus of control for future meaningful learning.

As the facilitator encourages adult learners to reflect on their experience, identify assumptions, and assess the relationships among the sociocultural influences on their educational activities and other biographical themes, multidisciplinary insights regarding adult learning can emerge. These insights may illuminate both the organized knowledge typical of formal education and the indigenous knowledge typical of experiential learning. In this process too, adults are empowered by learning how to learn and by assuming major responsibility for their own learning. As educators guide this process, they are empowered to recognize and make explicit their own beliefs regarding adult learning.

Collaborative Interpretation

Interpretation occupies a central place in the educational biography approach. As in action science, also known as action research or participatory research, interpretation is a shared task. It takes place through dialogue. Each oral and written narrative, which already embodies its author's interpretation, is submitted to a further interpretation by a small group of peers. The adult learners are both active partners and beneficiaries in this process. And educators also benefit from the resulting insights about adults' subjective views of their learning activities. Thus hermeneutics becomes a method of research, a method that is also inspired by the concepts of grounded theory and comprehensive sociology (discussed in later chapters).

Hermeneutic interpretation of subjective experience enables adult learners to discover how much their identity results from their learning experiences—that is, to what extent these experiences are a process for becoming oneself—and how much the dynamics of learning belong to the construction of their own identity. Following Ricoeur (1986), we can say that writing a narrative is an act of testimony about one's own identity. For adult educators, learning about their own process of learning is also a way to understand the more general process of their students' learning.

Adults can learn how to learn more effectively by reflecting on their experiences as actors in different contexts (Schön, 1987; Smith and Associates, 1990). In particular they may see how past experience shapes their relation to knowledge. If they have received bad grades in math in the past, for example, they may have understood that they should not choose a scientific curriculum. When they study psychology later in life, the early experience will lead them to expect difficulties in mastering statistics. A similar result will obtain from early bad experiences in any area of learning. As adult learners look back to their pasts, they also often discover social and cultural reasons for the schooling and vocational choices they have made. They grasp the interactive play between formal and experiential learning. Experiential learning disqualifies as well as qualifies formal learning. Conversely, many adults undervalue what they have learned from life experiences because it is not formal learning.

Educator coaching and peer exchange are valuable because many adults experience difficulty with such reflection. Through sharing their educational biographies with other learners, they gain both an affirmation of the uniqueness and diversity of others' educational journeys and an appreciation of the similar themes that emerge. However, some adults are reluctant to discuss their educational pasts when their memories of school are especially painful or when they have difficulty talking about themselves on any topic. This reluctance is found more among men and among both men and women with lower-class cultural backgrounds. This is one of the reasons the biographical approach to learning about learning requires a lot of trust among the members of a group. Interpretation of educational biographies could not take place successfully in, for example, a group made up of women refugees from different countries because they would have too many cultural differences. Most adults are not ready to share their lives with people they do not know or with people from dissimilar social backgrounds.

Subjectivity

A life history narrative is prepared by an individual author but shared with a group. It tells about an individual life, but family, school, peers and lovers, work life, and social involvements are always present. Students who work in a world of relationships (social workers, teachers, and nurses, for example) produce clearly psychodynamic interpretations of their educational biographies. But educational biography is not primarily a tool for better knowledge about adult development. It is not a new source of knowledge for adult psychology. An educational biography is an interpretation made by an adult about his or her life journey in learning, and it does not belong to the domain of psychology or sociology. Instead, it offers insight on what it means for an adult to become the subject of his or her life. Biographical testimonies are subjective testimonies in that they represent a process of "subjectivation." As Guy de Villers (1993) puts it, educational biography has a subjective effect (or in his terms, a "subject effect"). Adult students often realize through their narratives that whatever influences and dependencies characterize their individual journeys, they can still become authors of their lives.

The world of adult education has been invaded by psychology and recently by humanist psychology. Most adults interpret their lives in psychological terms. They diagnose superficially their needs and hopes. They attend a workshop or a lecture and believe their lives can change, or conversely, they realize after years of psychoanalysis that they had better remain who they are. However, educational biography as research process has for its object the *learning process* through which learners have built their lives. A French term, *formation*, is useful here: *formation* describes the alliance of formal and experiential learning that gives shape to an adult life. Life taking form, life entering into its form, the sculpture of life, all these expressions present sometimes in students' narratives refer to this theoretical object of educational biography. Seen in this light, educational biography needs a multidisciplinary analysis, just as education itself should be interdisciplinary and not merely a collection of disciplines.

Educational biography does not belong to psychology because it is basically subjective. And this subjectivity reflects the central theoretical question of education: Who is the subject of education? What is the locus or the focus of education if not the subject involved in a process of learning?

Emerging Trends

Educational biography is part of the growing volume of qualitative research in the social sciences. Disciplines such as psychology, sociology, and history have developed the practice of life history for such varied types of research as studies in gender, of aged adults, and of people on the margins of society. This resurgence follows the post–World War II period when quantitative, empirical research eclipsed the qualitative methods characteristic of anthropology and history and espoused by the Chicago School of sociology, which was producing case history studies of human development.

Today's reemergence of inquiry through life history reflects many influences. One such influence is the new ascendance of a life cycle perspective on people's lives, a perspective fostered by an aging population. National economic crises and contexts of unemployment have also obliged adults, especially young adults, to reconsider the specific biographical dimension of work life (Alheit, 1995). Modern life carries "mental demands" (Kegan, 1996) that oblige adults to work on self-guidance and self-knowledge. All these influences are opening new horizons for the world of adult education. As we educators discover more about adults' lives and ways of learning, the resulting dialogue can enrich our knowledge of ways to help adults guide their lives, including ways to empower them to guide their own learning. Educational biography is a vehicle through which students may gain such insights directly for themselves. And adult educators are enhancing learners' active search for meaning by such means as assisting learners to share stories about critical incidents in their lives, interacting with learners in a dialogical process, and helping learners link theory and practice (Hatch and Wisniewski, 1995; Merriam and Brockett, 1997). Attention given to the educational biographies of adult learners is also reinforcing the growing tendency to search for what is often called *clinical knowledge*. In contrast to scientific knowledge, clinical knowledge arises out of collaborative analysis of single cases that are considered meaningful. It corresponds to a theoretical look at critical situations from within. The different levels of analysis include the learner, the learner's relation with an educator or facilitator and with the group, the organizational setting, and such more symbolic levels of personal investment as the wish to change.

Finally, it is obvious that a variety of biographical approaches are emerging in the world of adult education as a result of increasing attention to self-directed learning. In the next two chapters, I describe some of these approaches along with a particular approach I have used and a closer look at the reasoning that supports the transformative learning process offered to adult learners by educational biography.

Chapter Two

Understanding Biographical Approaches to Learning

This chapter discusses the educational biography approach I have created and used in the context of my own teaching at the University of Geneva. In this chapter and the subsequent one, in addition to explaining the procedures I have used and my reasons for using them, I mention in broad outline the various ways in which practitioners might employ the educational biography approach.

I began using educational biographies as a means of conducting my own educational research. Thus I describe and discuss the educational biography methodology as a challenge for research. Adult educators who are willing to reflect deeply on how adults learn during their lives will find themselves inspired by the practice of educational biography.

Overview of the Educational Biography Seminar at the University of Geneva

At the University of Geneva a course structured around the creation of an educational biography is taught as a seminar for students majoring in education or psychology or those studying to be adult educators. The seminar covers two semesters of approximately fourteen weeks each; each seminar section has about twenty-five students and meets once a week for two hours. Students do much of their classroom work in small groups of six to eight, each group facilitated by a teaching assistant. Each student is expected to complete both an oral and a written life history narrative. The seminar progresses through the following phases.

Delivering information about the seminar. Before final registration, interested students are given information about the seminar requirements, organization, and plans for the academic year. Time is devoted to discussing the meaning of the commitment expected from each participant. Students are of course free to attend the seminar or not on the basis of this information.

Introducing the seminar. During the first three sessions, the teacher presents a theoretical and methodological introduction to educational biography. Students ask questions after each lecture, and the ensuing discussions give the teacher and the teaching assistants the opportunity to explain the theoretical background and procedures. They also mention their own area of research in the field of life history. And they describe the historical background of the life history approach as well as its different practices, including those applied to adult education. (The next chapter gives an overview of the references presented in this introduction.) The teacher explains how educational biography emerged as an field of training and research in education and distributes papers and articles on topics related to educational biography. The key dimensions discussed relate primarily to students' frequent resistance to learning from subjective implications (as opposed to what they consider objective findings) and their ability to contribute to the production of knowledge.

Initiating the small groups. The small groups of six to eight students are formed at random, but adjustments may then be made in order to avoid potential conflicts. Work on the oral narratives, written narratives, and evaluations takes place in these groups, facilitated by the teacher and the teaching assistants, during about twenty weeks of the two-hour seminars. Each group is allowed to reorganize the plan for these weeks in accord with the special needs of its members. Each group also establishes a written contract among its members during its first session. Issues such as discretion in sharing the narratives outside the group and regular attendance at the seminar are always addressed in this contract.

Before participants start their narratives, each is also expected to write a short paper explaining an issue he or she wishes to research through preparing a life history. Participants might have as an object of research the decision-making process in their lives, reasons for their difficulties with writing, how they deal with their intercultural background, or other questions about their own development or about applications to which the educational biography approach might contribute.

Delivering oral narratives. Each group devotes two hours to preparing for participants' oral narratives. Group members raise and discuss such questions as: What should we say, and what should we avoid in the narrative? Should we write out what we want to say in the oral presentation, or should we work only from notes? How should we collect the necessary information? Should we interview family members, friends, or former teachers? In the following meetings, two hours are devoted to each participant's oral narrative, about an hour of presentation and an hour of discussion; that is, one student in each group presents an oral narrative at each weekly seminar until all have done so. These presentations are audiotaped.

Preparing written narratives. In between preparing the oral and the written narratives the teacher and the class as whole discuss the process and style of writing an educational biography. Then, during the following weeks, each participant writes his or her narrative at home, using the tape of the oral version and any notes he or she may have taken during the oral presentation and discussion. This phase falls during the break between the semesters, in order to give students sufficient time to complete their written narratives.

Delivering commentaries. The next phase is devoted to commentary, or interpretation. Each participant is asked to choose one written narrative, read it carefully, and present a kind of analysis. Some guidelines are offered by the teacher and assistants. The main themes, structure, key learning experiences, and personal ways of thinking that give biography its meaning are especially taken into consideration. Participants may chose the narratives they wish to read, according to their own agendas and their desire to read one narrative more than another, or (to make things easier) the narratives may be randomly distributed. Each commentary is followed by group discussion of the analyzed narrative; like the oral narratives, each written narrative is analyzed and discussed over a two-hour seminar session. Although one person is the chief commentator, all the other students in the group are expected to participate in the discussion. During this time the teacher also reads for the first time all the written biographies.

Evaluating the process. An evaluation takes place during the last two seminar meetings. The teacher and assistants help the groups identify the main themes and key questions that were discussed. Later each group presents an oral or written report to the plenary in order to share the results of this attempt to summarize the elements of knowledge produced in each group. Each participant is also asked to write an evaluation of the process of educational biography. These evaluations are distributed to other members of the group and discussed in order to underline methodological viewpoints that will be mentioned later at the plenary session.

As mentioned, the whole process takes the full academic year. Sometimes, when time allows, teachers will share their own oral or written narratives with the group. Every student who has registered and fulfilled the assignment gets credit for the seminar.

Although I first wanted to make use of this methodology for the purpose of research, I soon had to recognize its impact on the learning process of the students. As Gaston Pineau (1980) noted, this method is very demanding: "the effort to make explicit an educational life history is a costly commitment which requires emotional commitment and awareness" (p. 1; my translation). I recognized that research and learning were two different aspects of the methodology. Even if the research results were sometimes disappointing, what the students learned through this research was a benefit of the process. The researchers did not have the same status as the students. They had their own research questions, but the results of their research depended on the students' quality of participation. At first, I favored the specific research questions raised by my colleagues and assistants. Today, I ask every student in the seminar to prepare his or her own questions in order to participate in both the training program and the research project. This common pursuit of both research and learning makes the methodology of educational biography specific to the field of adult education and not an application of social science.

Let's look at some important factors in this seminar more closely, particularly the aim of the research and the process of analysis.

Choosing the Object of Research

From the beginning the object of research was conceived as an interpretation by the participants themselves of their educational journey. Two main questions were raised: a general question, Out of my entire educational life history what do I select as important to my learning process? and a more specific question, What has the role of schooling been in my learning process? I use *learning process* to translate the French word *formation* (a word that exists also in English but is not used in reference to the formative effects of education as it is in French). In German, the word used would be *Bildung*. As I understand this learning process, its dimensions are so encompassing that a biographical narrative can mention only some of its aspects. There is no way to grasp the whole process in a narrative. Thus the main question arose because the educational biography is necessarily a fragment of a more global life history. It is always a partial interpretation of a part of a life history.

For research purposes I first asked the students to follow an outline. I wanted them all to focus on the same themes. It took me a couple of years to understand that the way a narrative was constructed was part of its meaning. By imposing a structure, I selected the information my students could use, and I forced them to construct their narratives according to my own research purpose. They must have felt this bias because they requested that they be free to ask their own questions about their life histories and to prepare narratives directed to their own research purposes.

Of course the objects students choose are still greatly influenced by my general research purpose. They know of the work that has been done before because I present my research in the first phase of the seminar and they have read some of the material I have published. It is nevertheless important that they have the freedom to interpret this general research purpose and to present their educational biographies according to their own interpretations.

Another factor affecting the research is that the biographical work takes place in a group setting. The participants address themselves to other adults whom they learn to know and trust. They construct their narratives with an eye to both the openness and the limitations of the interaction between themselves and these others. They are also attending a class at the university, and the written narrative is necessarily influenced by this academic context. Moreover, the difference between the freedom they have in the content and structure of the oral and the written biographical narratives and the more formal content and structure of the presentations or papers they have to produce in other classes always strikes them and can be considered a learning dimension of this approach.

When, after a couple of years, I could identify specific processes as being a typical part of the learning process of adults, like the struggle for autonomy in regard to one's family of origin or the construction of a vocational choice, I was tempted to ask my students for a narrative centered on one of these processes. Again I rejected this method as being an imposition on them of my research object. I wanted them to restructure, on their own terms, the object of my research as a guide for the construction of their narrative. Methodologically speaking, I consider this reinterpretation essential for writing narratives that are meaningful in describing the learning process and, consequently, for achieving my research purpose.

Preparing for Narratives and Delivering the Oral Narrative

The methodological debate about the life history approach is mainly centered on the narrative and its interpretation. After dealing for years with questions related to this debate, I have come to the conclusion that the only relevant question is that of the purpose. I am now mostly concerned with the viability of my approach as it relates to the purpose with which I want to deal. The norms of the social sciences are not too relevant for educational biographies. I am not taking a sample; I do not consider statistical treatment of the information, what others might call data, really feasible. I do not even think it accurate to use the term data, because in this approach we are in the world of interpretation from the beginning to the end. The dynamic of the research process is the central methodological question that is being considered.

The educational biography is always an interpretation of part of an adult's life history. Thus comparison between biographies is not necessarily useful. What matters is to facilitate the interpretation of first the oral and then the written versions of each biography. As I mentioned, an outline is a support that might misdirect students as they prepare their oral narratives. Even raising questions, as one might in a preliminary interview with the participant, might mislead that person's effort. In brief, the learning that occurs during the work of preparing the narrative is a condition of the quality of the research process, and this has convinced me to give quasi-total freedom to students in preparing their narratives.

The quality of the oral narrative also depends greatly on the quality of the listening offered to the speaker. The process requires deep trust among the participants. The two hours allotted for this presentation and the subsequent discussion might seem short, but the preparation could require several days. Some participants have said that as soon as they begin the seminar they also start the process of structuring their narratives. What they present is generally what they believe has to be said for an understanding of their own research object. Each participant works alone. Again, in order not to influence biography content, the teacher does not offer any aid in the development of the narrative.

Being timid, some say orally what they have previously written out; others have only notes in front of them. Again, everybody has to find his or her own style, with only one condition which is the time limit on delivering the narrative. The articles and papers students read at the beginning of the seminar are intended to help them reflect on the meaning of the content they are progressively selecting. By showing them what has been done before, it gives them a better idea of what is expected from them and what might be useful to them.

Several methodological questions could be asked about the interpretive process. One of the most frequent questions raised by students has to do with the difference between educational biography and psychotherapy. Participants who have previously been helped with therapy are less afraid to talk about themselves in personal terms. However, the social context in which educational biographies are delivered differs greatly from the interpersonal encounter of psychotherapy. Participants who have little experience in working on personal development are more surprised by the approach. They soon realize, as they listen to the first oral narratives, that working on an educational journey differs from dealing with the conflictual dimensions of personal life. There is no doubt some similarity between educational biography and psychotherapy, but as a teacher conducting the approach, I insist on the differences, and I want the participants to recognize the differences between the educational side of a life history and the psychological blocking or suffering of a personal life. These differences have to be clarified at some time during the group work by the teacher. And I remain watchful in order to lead the discussion to the object of research if necessary. Generally speaking, the encounter during the discussion is strong, but the group has a common and external object of reflection in the general research object of the learning process. Also, the sociological or cultural dimensions of the biography for each participant point to directions of thought beyond the psychological.

Deepening Analysis with the Written Narrative

Once each member of each group of six to eight participants has had the opportunity to present his or her oral narrative, a new phase of the seminar starts with the written narratives. Some students base their written versions on their oral versions. Some students have developed since they gave their oral narratives, and they produce quite different written versions. Some students have new interpretations of their life histories. As one participant remarked, "the written version has helped me to look at my life from a different perspective." There is a big variation in texts, but in contrast with the oral versions they have in common a more formal style with fewer details and illustrations.

Asking students to prepare both oral and written educational biographies gives them an opportunity to deepen their analyses, and the final texts represent choices among possible levels of interpretation. Also the written text confirms what the oral narrative has already revealed: an educational biography is an expression of the way adults understand their lives and think about their education. It is not realistic to expect from the participants something other than what they can produce. The norms of evaluation are different than in other academic classes. The final version is neither right nor wrong. It has to be considered a testimony of the meaning an adult is able to give to his or her life experiences.

The quality of the written biographies naturally varies. Some can be considered good literature. The style is often moving and colorful, better than the average university paper. Many students who were always afraid of papers they had to write have discovered the pleasure of writing as they prepare their biographies. The quest for the right word to describe a personal experience becomes important. Writing educational biographies also reduces the distance between a concrete experience and its formal presentation or between what is considered intimate and what is considered public. For many women this search for expression is especially meaningful because they have been obliged by the dominant culture to keep quiet and to reduce their exchanges to private, interpersonal comments. The biographical assignment creates a challenge that they often enjoy immensely. Generally speaking, the writing of an educational biography introduces a central understanding about the social and personal aspects of the learning process to participants as they try to present the social dimension of a life experience whose truth depends on personal authenticity.

Continuing the Interpretation

During the first year of my research, after the students had discussed their narratives and I had read them all, I set some categories of analysis and suggested to the students some empirical ways to analyze the content. Some students strongly resisted my proposal because they felt that this kind of analysis would have a weakening effect on the whole approach and make it insipid. They also felt short on time and decided, after a general analysis of the work done, that they would meet for another year but in two different groups. The members of one group decided to revisit their biographies and, instead of analyzing the content, to deepen a selected part of the biography with a second narrative. The members of the other group decided to deal with their narratives in terms of some specific themes of theoretical analysis, such as the way adults regulate change in their lives. These two ways of going further with the analysis of the narratives have now been used by participants several times: students either work on a second narrative in order to deepen their interpretation of a portion of their life history and or they work on generative themes coming out of a first reading of the narratives.

I have tried to develop the content analysis of the narratives in many directions. The issue of content analysis in academic circles is loaded with methodological questions. The scientific discipline of analysis is associated closely with quantitative data. Research is traditionally associated with proof more than with hypothetical assertions. The idea that research generates general hypotheses is typically not accepted. At different phases of my research, then, I have tried to build a typology, or I have hoped to find some statistical clues that would reduce the amount of information that needed to be collected. Yet I came to the conclusion that I still defend today that the methodology of educational biography must be a mode of reflection rather than an if-then statement and proof.

I drew this conclusion after years of trying to find the right content analysis. I selected the biographies, trying to build clusters according to age, school background, or profession. After reading the narratives several times, I tried to restructure the texts according to chronological categories or life events. These attempts, even if they have helped me to master the content of the narratives, did not lead me very far. Progressively, I understood that everything I was doing in order to compare the narratives was in many ways resulting in transferring their meaning to an objective other than the one for which they were made. For example, comparing the content of a group of narratives made me aware of some processes, which I call mini-processes, that occur within much larger learning process, such as the process of leaving the family of birth, of constructing a vocational life, and of achieving cultural rootedness. If I had pursued this line, I would have done my research according to the classical models of social science and from an epistemological position inadequate for the adult and continuing education context in which the educational biography approach is used.

Researchers in the field of life history and educational biography have made use of several types of content analysis. Pineau (Pineau and Marie-Michèle, 1983) has taken a single biography and analyzed it with the help of its author and of general categories. A. Michaël Huberman (1990) has built a qualitative approach that is very useful for dealing correctly with the types of information collected. Sociologists such as Didier Demazière and Claude Dubar (1997) have also used qualitative content analysis with biographies. Peter Alheit's book (1994) on the life histories of unemployed young people, recently translated into English, is an example of a careful analysis of biographical interviews inspired by the idea of *grounded theory* developed by Barney G. Glaser and Anselm L. Strauss (1967).

Bertaux (1980), in his sociological work, has defended the idea of a "saturation effect" in content analysis, in order to provide a scientific justification for generating hypotheses. He means that after a researcher collects and analyzes a cluster of biographies, the repetition of themes or recurrent way of telling stories that the researcher finds has the effect of allowing him or her to conclude with a hypothesis. It is not a proof but a solid hypothesis based on this saturation effect. Moreover, sometimes one narrative may be enough to point to a theme that may then assert itself more strongly through the saturation effect.

However, it is my finding that each text has to be taken as a whole. Omitting to consider some part of the content might distort the meaning of a narrative. My final decision has been to keep each narrative separate and intact, to underline each narrative's specific character. By identifying the main themes of each biography, however, I also remain open to more general biographical trends that could be illuminating for educational practice.

I also decided at one point to take the link between the training of adult educators and the research on adult learning more seriously in my seminars, making the content analysis part of the interactive dimension of the research in the seminar. As described earlier in the overview, each narrative is read by all members of the group and discussed on the basis of a first analysis made by a member who is not the author. Both the author and the participant who presents the analysis explain how they have proceeded and on what basis they have constructed or analyzed the text. The discussion is supposed to enrich both the interpretation of the life history offered by the author and the hypothesis the author makes about the learning process as the object of his or her research.

The interpretation of a narrative is an endless process that might modify over and over again the content to be analyzed. Those students who have written a new version of their educational biography a year or two after the first attempt have experienced this firsthand. Both versions are subject to an interactive dynamic in which the value of the interpretation depends a great deal on the capacity of the participants to interpret their own lives as well as the lives of others. In that sense, the initial work done in building the biography is a condition for a valuable final interpretation.

However, students are so emotionally attached to their narratives that it is difficult for them to remain open to another object of research. They deal with their own process of learning through life more than with the general process of adult learning. They lack the time and distance for a deeper investment. In order for learning and research to take place within the same process, it is necessary to combine not only learning and research but learner and researcher. Yet, typically, the teacher and those few students who are writing a thesis are the only persons involved who have the time, the distance, and the ability to be researchers.

It is of course as a researcher that the researcher is particularly at risk of falling into the trap of looking at the narratives as empirical data and following a methodology influenced by the traditional models of social science. At a stage of scientific research when hermeneutics is more and more recognized as a methodology for interpreting qualitative data in the form of recorded and transcribed interviews, it is important to underline once again the specificity of the texts produced by the methodology of educational biography. A student's written narrative is not similar to another text and cannot be considered a final product. What the author says does not cover what he or she could tell. As I described earlier, a question of research has to be thought, stated, and made explicit by each participant in a short paper before the oral narratives are delivered. The oral as well as the written narratives are discussed in general before and in particular after their presentation to the group. They become objects of analysis as participants become socialized within the group. The researcher has listened, read, and discussed with the participants for more than twenty-five weeks. The researcher's knowledge of the author plays a role in his or her interpretation of the narrative. Thus the educational biography approach delivers more than a text for the interpretation of a life story.

Reasons to Be Satisfied

After some years I have had to recognize that my first intuition was right. Educational biography is an interesting tool for reflecting on the learning process and for gaining a better understanding of the way adults educate themselves. Many adult educators are attracted by the idea of using biographical approach, and many new variations on this approach have been developed since I first started using life histories in adult education. It is time to seek a better understanding of the success of this approach.

First of all it is important to emphasize that adults are fascinated by this approach that examines their personal life history as a whole and gives meaning to the learning moments and events they would not at first glance have considered instances of learning. Adults have to put together aspects of their life that society has divided into pieces. In an educational biography, schooling, for example, cannot be separated from significant moments of socialization or commitment to groups such as religious organizations. Moreover, generally speaking, the bad memories are tied in with the joys of life. Chronological breaks also need to be bridged. Parents, for example, are mostly present in the narratives as they are remembered from the authors' childhood and then again as they enter old age or die.

As adults investigate the global scene of their life history the meaning of their lives is transformed. We are accustomed in our society to having our lives broken up among divergent contexts and organizations and to living only portions of ourselves at a time. The need to keep a job obliges many professionals to hide their political or religious convictions. People often travel to realize their dreams and forget their daily lives. The media, by imposing a cultural life dominated by intensity and emotion, have a tendency to reinforce lives fractured between pleasure and boredom. The biographical approach allows adults a new way of reflecting about themselves and the world in which they live.

The educational biography also allows learners and researchers a space for a subjectivity that has been denied by the scientific norms of social science. At this time when criticism of scientific rigidity is allowed, the life history approach is making a comeback. Subjectivity is no longer seen as opposed to quantitative findings. What needs to be stressed is the variety of avenues through which thinking can take place. Empirical data and scientific proof are not the only things by far upon which we can reflect. I have already insisted that there are limits to the general categories of analysis that can be separated from the context and the person for which these categories might have meaning. In the biographical approach, respect for the subjectivity of the author and the commentator is a basic principle for successful construction and interpretation of the narrative. In many ways the narrative is meaningful because it is subjective. That is, the author expresses himself or herself as the subject of a learning process and not only in terms of a role he or she played in the past (as a child related to a family, for example) or in the present (perhaps as a worker or as a citizen). Another way to view this subjectivity is as the global understanding of the author produced by the biography. This subjectivity is not the same thing as the contemporary expression of individualism. The comments of Michel de Certeau (1981) writing about the Freudian use of biography are relevant here: "Freudianism introduces a new biographical approach opposed to individualism as it is stated by modern psychology. With the use of this tool, Freudianism denounces the assumption of a liberal society. It replaces individualism with a historical perspective: the system of tragedy" (p. 135; my translation). Tragedy here refers to the Greek idea of destiny.

This principle of subjectivity, which I consider to be a condition for the authenticity of the educational biography approach, is not easy to accept. The students are often surprised by the freedom of expression this approach gives to them. They have always associated education with institutional rules and standards like scheduled programs and norms of evaluation. In their view, learning is completely enclosed in an organizational setting. Being a good student seems more important to them than being a good learner. I have the impression that by making learning the focus and object of the life history, the educational biography opens a new epistemological perspective for learners and researchers.

This understanding of the subjectivity of learning explains why I want to combine research and learning in the educational biography approach. The organizational norms of research are as strong as the organizational norms of learning. As long as I, as the teacher-researcher, kept the power to raise the questions of research and to deal with content analysis, I did not give the students a chance to contribute to the research. It was when I asked the students to explain their own questions of research and to reflect and then define hypotheses on the basis of a content analysis of the package of biographies that came out of each group that I really understood the vital importance of relating learning and research closely. Without research, learning leads to a report more than to reflection. Without learning, research reduces to a commonplace the personal content of a biography, failing to take advantage of the personal interpretation of the author. For example, the idea that a life history takes its structure from a personal conflict that the author is trying to solve (and perhaps has been dealing with for all of his or her life) came from a student's content analysis of a group of biographies. Of course teachers have to remain realistic. Most students do not contribute much theoretical material; nevertheless I consider their subjective perspective to be a condition of their better understanding of the adult learning process.

Toward a Plurality of Biographical Approaches

I have used educational biographies mainly in the context of university teaching and teacher training. My colleagues Matthias Finger and Christine Josso have both contributed to the enlargement of my initial approach: Finger (1989) by using the educational biography to identify the consciousness-raising process and to define the central questions for a more empirical research project, Josso (1991) by presenting with courage and subtlety her own educational biography in order to explain what she calls "the knowledge process."

Some years ago Finger, Josso, and I decided to explore the biographical approach by working with a population of adult educators outside the context of the university. Adult educator training programs are developing rapidly in universities, and yet no one knows exactly what level of competency a person requires to be an adult educator. We wanted to learn about this competency. We decided to choose adult educators who could be considered pioneers in the field and who had years of experience. Most of those who committed to our project had been among the first to hold their positions; thus they had had the opportunity to define the content of their jobs. We used the biographical approach in order to reconstruct with them the process through which their competency had been established. We adapted our existing methodology of educational biography to a five-day workshop and explored this approach with four different groups of adult educators. Obviously, time was more of a constraint than it is at the university level, and it was necessary to strike some bargains over the workshop plan and the requirements of the research. We also could not expect a high-quality commitment.

Later I give a fuller picture of the results of this research. Here my focus is the significance of the subjectivity in such biographical projects. For example, each educator had for a professional profile the profile he or she was really looking for, and the qualifications they recognized as central to their job were totally connected with their life histories. In short, this biographical method is rich with possibilities because it can be modified according to different research purposes and training program objectives.

Of course fields other than adult education could be explored. Here for example are three contexts in which I hope some day to develop new biographical approaches. A biographical approach in the context of maintaining one's health could help participants discover how everyone, throughout his or her life, has learned to take care of himself or herself or to handle a handicap or a chronic disease. A biographical approach in the political context could help participants learn how they built their political consciousness or by what process they became involved in political action. A biographical approach in the context of religious belief could help participants learn how they have built their faith or religious belief and how conviction and skepticism alternate in a life history. Such research could largely contribute to necessary knowledge about medical patients. It could be helpful in a time of political disengagement and individualism. It could produce a better understanding of the place of faith and the building of a value system in the course of an adult life that would help all kinds of individuals who are facing a crisis in their cultural environment.

Indeed, for me, in these and similar contexts, the biographical approach is the only relevant methodology because it offers direct access to the knowledge coming out of people's experience and the language in which they speak about it. Participatory research is shown again to be an epistemological issue.

An Approach Full of Traps

I have found that although the educational biography approach is full of satisfactions, it is also full of opportunities for missteps. Personal reflection on the questions posed in this section may help practitioners avoid these snares.

The biographical narrative belongs to the world of meaning and reflection. It does not have the accuracy of a fact or a figure such as one's date of birth or length of professional involvement. Is it still possible to talk about data if the content of a narrative varies according to the context and the group in which it has been presented? Given the power of scientific norms, is it necessary to take the time and energy to defend the methodology of educational biography, or is it a lost battle to begin with?

In our research with adult educators outside the standard university program, Josso and I have asked the participants to share their curricula vitae with each other. At the university, because the students in the seminar have met each other already, we do not feel this step is necessary. But I recognize that in both groups, group members' knowledge of each other gives the narratives a kind of implicit reality. I would not conduct the biographical approach in a workshop where the participants did not know anything about each other and could not be given enough time to prepare their narratives well. Preparing a life history opens the door to imaginative interpretation of life events. Is it then necessary to verify what has been said or written? Is the discussion of a narrative among the members of the group a guarantee of its truthfulness? Is it important for the leader of the group to be careful about the authenticity of the narrative? Are these difficulties similar to the ones a researcher has to deal with in considering the truthfulness of answers to questionnaires and other more empirical data? Should researchers and teachers use a biographical approach as a first phase of research that could lead to a questionnaire with a larger sample and statistical verification? Each one of these questions should be raised, and the answers offered should be theoretically sound and free from scientific dogmas.

Is the biographical approach usable by any adult, or does it require some basic ability? I had to face this problem when I felt that one woman in a group of adult educators was totally unable to think about her life in a genetic way. In addition, one must consider the participants' ages and thus the amount of experience to which they can refer in their biographies. Why are some life histories more meaningful than others for the person who is listening? Why did Pineau (Pineau and Marie-Michèle, 1983) chose Marie-Michèle as a subject and Catani (Catani and Mazé, 1982) Aunt Suzanne? I have often told myself that by working mostly with university students I have had too homogeneous a population. It is, however, difficult to establish a set of criteria for selecting the "right" population. I must confess that some narratives I have read are more meaningful for me than others. But it would be almost impossible to explain the reasons for my reaction. Therapeutic work done beforehand might help participants prepare their biographies, but it could also deflect participants from making discoveries about their learning. A lack of intellectual ability might also restrict the interpretation of a life history, but the contrary condition might distort the narrative with too much reasoning. The quality of the discussion of the oral version has a certain impact on the written text, but again it would be extremely difficult to identify the conditions of a good group. I see two issues that have to be respected: time and personal commitment, which are closely related. The dual learning and research perspective requires that a great deal of time should be devoted to the construction of the purpose for research; the creation of an appropriate climate in the overall group; and the preparation, delivery, and discussion of the narratives, both oral and written. This should be emphasized to anyone who is starting to use the biographical approach.

The question of the qualifications the person who leads the overall group should have is not easy to answer. However, it seems clear to me that people in charge of any kind of session that uses biography should know what they are looking for in terms of research and learning. They should have the intellectual ability to be ahead of the group in its reflection. They should also master group dynamics and use them for the purposes of research and learning. They should facilitate the work by setting an example of good listening. They should be forward with their own remarks and questions yet not take too much of the group's time or introduce their own norm for the discussion. They must respect the time required and allot a reasonable length of time for the task of preparing and discussing the narratives. The person in charge has finally to choose the right way to bring students' present work to closure and to determine whether it makes sense to begin a new phase of biographical work that might take some months or another year or whether a set of learners are not ready for another phase even though they may be having difficulty breaking off their present effort. It is up to leader as researcher to know what he or she wants to write or publish on the basis of the work done in the overall group and the written narratives available. In some cases the group, or some members of it, might like to share the responsibility of producing an article.

What must experienced educators do with the participants who want to start their own educational biography groups and who decide to imitate what they have done with the experienced practitioner? Is it necessary to control all efforts inspired by the educational biography approach? What, again, is the competence required to help learners use the approach? As I wrote (Dominicé, 1995) in a chapter of a book recently published by the Life History and Biographical Research network of the European Society for Research in the Education of Adults, a network of practitioners engaged in a constant discussion about the educational biography approach has the potential to support competence in the field in a way that might not be possible at the local level due to rivalry. However, I would add this possibly simplistic comment: there is no way to avoid misuse of the biographical method. All of us in adult education should do our work seriously and be open to discussion. This is the best we can do to maintain the quality of work we want to do.

Quoting from Narratives in Research

Finally, the researcher or participant who wishes to use another person's biographical narrative in some way faces an ethical question. Once the narratives have been prepared and distributed, what may be done with them outside the small group? In my seminars the author of each oral narrative is the only one who has the tape of his or her presentation; however, the written texts circulate among the members of the group. This requires a lot of trust from everyone, and the group must agree upon a social contract that governs how they will respect each other's texts. This contract, signed by everyone in the group gives sole responsibility to the author for sharing his or her narrative with people outside the group. The narratives otherwise belong exclusively to the members of the group for use within the group.

The researcher who wishes to use narrative content in his or her publications is not involved in this contract. However, because I have had difficult experiences myself in the past when I published quotations from educational biographies, I now follow the rule of obtaining permission from an author before quoting his or her material. Seminar participants are rather sensitive on this issue, but they have the right to be sensitive, because most of the time in our society the personal is among the secret things of life.

The debate over quoting is sometimes taken a step further. Even with the agreement of the authors, should the researcher quote at all? Material extracted from a narrative may present a distorted view of the research of its author. Josso decided that she was responsible only for her own biography. That is why she never quotes anybody. I have used extracts from narratives with the permission of their authors because I felt that offering an interpretation of the way life histories could contribute to a better theoretical understanding of adult learning was the right thing to do and that these extracts were helpful in that endeavor. However, I admit this understanding is only one function of the biographical approach, which also explains why I have thought it necessary to make public my entire approach to life history in adult education. In any case this is an ethical issue that adult educators and researchers must never neglect to address with learners. Discussion of it also gives the students a better idea of a difficulty that might arise in any participative research. Finally, it underlines the difference I have described between educational biography and autobiography.

Summary

This chapter has presented the educational biography approach as I initiated it at the University of Geneva some years ago. In reaction against the narrowness of the exclusively empirical and statistical approaches of the last decades, a variety of biographical approaches have now appeared in the world of adult education. The growing networks of adult education researchers tend to give value to this recent methodology.

The educational biography contributes to participatory research in which the life history, viewed through the individual's formal and informal education, becomes a source of information that leads the individual and other participants to an understanding of the stages of learning through which his or her personal knowledge is acquired.

The educational biography is first prepared in the form of an oral narrative presented and discussed in small groups. This first narrative leads to the main themes that are developed in a new written version that matures over the remaining weeks of the seminar. This text does not follow an imposed scheme. The way it is structured should be considered an expression of its content.

Each text is analyzed by the author's small group, and one participant has the task of presenting an analysis that focuses the group discussion. After this stage the group becomes a kind of research group, working to find hypotheses that can enlighten the interactions that affect learning.

This methodology, which takes place in the context of a university, is not the only approach. Many shorter approaches have been developed lately for use in the training of trainers. By looking at the way they have learned what they know, adult educators become more sensitive to the ways other adults learn. When educational biographies are prepared by clusters of individuals with some common denominator (for example, the clientele of adult education), all the hearers and readers of the narratives share on at least one level a common language and the culture, which fosters their learning. This explains why the educational biography approach could be successfully adapted to a variety of groups, such as patients or churchgoers, and used for a variety of purposes.

Chapter Three

From Life History
to Educational Biography

The narrating of life histories has a long history of wide use. Furthermore, in the social sciences, ideas and practices do not come from nowhere. They have their own life history, to which any author is necessarily indebted. This chapter discusses the evolving literature on the use of biographies for various purposes but particularly for understanding adult development and learning. First, I outline the history of the approach and then I look at some common themes and trends around which biographies are organized and the literature related to them. Readers who are uninterested in this historical perspective may proceed to the next chapters, and perhaps return to this one after reading about the practical applications of biography.

A History of Life History

Life history has a long history. Several sources mention the genesis of biographical approaches. Among these sources are the seven-volume German *Geschichte des Autobiographie* (Misch, 1907) and the fifteen-volume English *University Library of Autobiography* (F. Tyler Daiels Co., 1918). Written life stories, according to some recent studies, existed in Greek culture five centuries before Christ, under the generic title *bios*. Ten centuries later, the word biography appeared, again in Greek. It was also used in Latin one century before Christ. Pineau and Legrand give a brief historical view on the use of the word biography in their book *Les Histoires de Vie*

(1993, pp. 20-36). The writing of autobiography in our modern sense emerged in the eighteenth century, although personal documents and diaries from early to recent times offer a variety of biographical texts. From Augustine to Rousseau, confessions were a style of writing that was close to the more recent practice of autobiography. Some medieval authors, such as Abelard, are also known for their use of personal life history. Montaigne's *Essays* might also be considered a form of autobiography. Spiritual meditation and exercises to achieve self-knowledge are part of Western culture and appeared long before the techniques of humanist psychology. Ignatius of Loyola's personal diary is an example.

Philippe Lejeune (1971, 1980) has done a magnificent analysis of autobiography as a field of literature, describing how this new phenomenon of narrating and publishing one's own personality developed in Western Europe from the middle of the eighteenth century. Today, biographies and autobiographies of noted statesmen, popular politicians, movie stars, and famous people in sports and other fields are selling millions of copies. In such varied forms as personal documents, diaries, commemorations, films, and now CD-ROMs, biographies reach a large public. There is also a growing trend to publish the life stories of people belonging to certain groups of social interest, such as elderly rural women or prisoners, employing the help of another person to turn these testimonies into written narratives. Of course many people have kept personal diaries without ever thinking about publishing them. Lejeune has recently created an association that has already collected hundreds of hitherto unpublished autobiographies for publication.

The methodology of life history is also being used by various social sciences. Due to the work of some prominent sociologists, such as Paul Lazarsfeld after World War II, the empirico-analytical model for collecting data eclipsed the qualitative tradition of participatory methodology coming out of the Chicago School of sociology. Now, however, new life history experiments have emerged and have stimulated the further emergence of educational biography. For example, life history has been used as a research tool by anthropologists such as Oscar Lewis (1961), who greatly contributed to the dissemination of the methodology. The psychoanalyst Erik Erikson (1963) has also used the methodology of life history in his work on psychobiography and the concept of the life cycle. Italian sociologist Franco Ferrarotti (1983) has used it for the study of families. In addition, narratives are being analyzed as historical documents by historians and are being used by psychologists interested in guidance and counseling. These different sources offer a theoretical and methodological background for those working on specific approaches in the field of adult education.

In the 1980s, in part given the stimulation of such sources, a group of sociologists organized an international association that sought to revive the life history approach for various applications. These European scholars published information on the phases of the development of the life history approach, from the time of the Chicago School around 1920 (see, for example, Thomas and Znaniecke, [1918] 1974) to the decline of this approach when quantitative methods dominated sociology. For example, a special issue of the *Cahiers Internationaux de Sociologie* (1980) presented several interesting articles on the development and decline and new potential of life histories. Daniel Bertaux, a sociologist in Paris, has been especially active in this activity (see, for example, Bertaux, 1980).

Going beyond the history and potential of the method, an Italian sociologist working in Paris, Maurizio Catani (1978; Catani and Mazé, 1982) has underlined how much the methodology of life history involves relationships between the researcher and the object of his or her research. For Catani (1978), "creating a social life history is primarily a question of relationship" (my translation). Ferrarotti (1983) has also indicated that the life history approach has not only methodological but epistemological implications, remarking, for example, that "if every individual is the singular reappropriation of a social and historical universality, we can come to know the social sphere on the basis of the irreducible specificity of an individual practice" (p. 51; my translation). Matthias Finger (1984), in his book on biography and hermeneutics, has also underlined the philosophical heritage of life history methodology in the work of such authors as the nineteenth-century German philosopher Wilhelm Dilthey and the methodology's connection with German sociologist Jurgen Habermas's concept of emancipation.

In the field of adult and continuing education, however, the life history approach was largely ignored, until, in the Canadian and European French-speaking world, Gaston Pineau and I did pioneering work to identify the possible contributions of life history to adult education and to build an appropriate methodology. Educational biography emerged out of this work in the 1980s. Since then various approaches have developed within educational biography along with the expansion of adult and continuing education. For example, the educational biography methodology is now used in a procedure for educational needs assessment to identify adults' educational expectations.

The creation of ASIHVIF (International Association for Life History Applied to Adult Education), an international network of adult educators and researchers in the field of adult education in French-speaking countries, has also stimulated this emergence of a plurality of biographical approaches. In France, for example, many directions have been explored. Life history approaches have been used as part of a reentry process for jobless workers and as a step in adult guidance and counseling. In the context of universities such as the University of Montreal, Catholic University of Louvain-la-Neuve (in Belgium), and University of Paris-Dauphine, the biographical approach has served the purpose of clarifying learners' needs and building a curriculum that takes participants' life histories into account. More recently, other members of this network have explored the life history approach with specific populations, such as alcoholics, prisoners, and rural women.

A similar network of individuals and institutions focused on the life history approach in social sciences applied to adult education has been created in the context of ESREA (European Society for Research in the Education of Adults), and as mentioned in the

Preface, five annual conferences have already taken place. Whereas ASIHVIF is a French-speaking network, ESREA is multicultural and has been important in bringing together the research that has taken place across Europe in the last decade. Peter Alheit, a German sociologist, and Wilhelm Mader, a psychoanalyst, have been especially active in Germany. Alheit has published a number of books on the life histories of workers' leaders and active trade unionists, using this approach as both a testimony to the individual subject's past life and a picture of working life in industrial areas. As Alheit (1992) says: "An autobiographical recourse necessarily touches upon the social identity aspect. We do not simply learn from biographical stories just for ourselves and our life-worlds; we gain insights into culture, society, and history" (p. 199). According to Alheit, we in the social sciences are now facing a new biographical challenge: "Biography itself has become a learning ground where transitions must be anticipated and where identity possibly is but the result of difficult learning processes. Life's course apparently seems to become a kind of unplanned 'laboratory' that serves to develop capabilities which provisionally do not figure in any curriculum" (pp. 187–188). Mader (1992) has worked with elderly people using guided autobiography. Women and education is another main theme that has been much studied. Cultural and intellectual contexts have strongly influenced the work done in different parts of Europe, and this ESREA network is still functioning as a place of intercultural dialogue.

Most of the remainder of this chapter focuses on the use of life history for some kind of adult education and outlines its main trends as they appear in the literature. Any information about adult life may help adult and continuing education become more responsive to adults' needs and expectations. However, I give particular attention to studies that address educational objectives in the use of biography. Sometimes this objective is mainly the validation of experiential learning. I also have selected works that offer broad theoretical contributions.

Selected Versions of Biography

At this level of generalization, I take into consideration three categories of studies regarding biographical approaches: those in the social and human sciences, those in the social and human sciences applied to adult education, and those focused specifically on educational biography. The discussion is organized according to some dominant themes in these categories of approaches.

The authors I mention should be taken as only a selection of those whose contributions I consider meaningful in the field of life history and, especially, educational biography. Certainly, I could have given more attention to the historical or sociocultural context surrounding the emergence of educational biography, but my main objective is to help the reader locate the theoretical framework and the methodology of educational biography. The main references are European, but I have tried to mention similar work done in the United States.

Educational biography belongs to a growing theoretical and methodological trend in the social and human sciences. In many ways I have borrowed ideas and approaches that I have reinterpreted for my own research purpose. However, I must underline the differences between applying human and social sciences to an analysis of adult life stages, as discussed later among these versions of biography, and building a specific framework in order to better understand the inner dynamics of the ways adults learn and give shape to their life. Adult education is not a bounded scientific discipline. Our way of thinking about adult education has to be multidisciplinary.

Sociology offers one epistemological background for using biographical methodology. It has been used in the study of aging, for example (Lalive d'Epinay, 1996). Martin Kohli (1986) also wrote several articles on later life based on a methodology of life history. Because the population in the Western world is on average aging, funding has become available for research in gerontology, and many studies have been done recently using biographical sources to examine later life. Such sociological literature is helpful as long as it can inspire conceptual frameworks for understanding adult learning.

Psychological studies of adult development have also often used biographical data in a variety of ways. Clinical psychology and efforts to achieve psychoanalytical awareness also use a biographical approach. Moreover, many students have been influenced by psychotherapy, whether individually or in a group, and the vocabulary they use when they talk about themselves seems to reflect the language used during their therapy.

In the following sections, I sketch some themes that are important in studies of adults and that can clarify and conceptualize the relationships between sociology and educational biography and between psychology and educational biography, relationships adult educators need to understand as they develop their own way of thinking about their practice.

Immigration and Cultural Identity

Immigration and cultural identity was a major theme in the earliest social and human sciences studies that relied on a biographical methodology. Thomas and Znaniecke's 1918 *The Polish Peasant in Europe and America*, a book about immigrants in Chicago, was a pioneering study. William Thomas, an American sociologist and one of the early members of the Chicago School of sociology, was trained in Germany at the end of the nineteenth century, when epistemology was at the center of debate. *The Polish Peasant* was a two-thousand-page survey of the cultural and social problems of interethnicity, such as the urban violence attributed to immigrants to Chicago. At the time Chicago was sometimes called "the third Polish city." Thomas met Florian Znaniecke in Poland. They worked together for years, each in his own country, and then, to obtain intercultural views, they traded places, the Pole went to America and the American went to Poland. After Znaniecke returned to Poland, he was instrumental in establishing a Polish

School of sociology that gave priority to the methodology of biography. At the time of Thomas and Znaniecke's study in the then new field of sociology, there was a real concern for joining theoretical analysis with practical action. This perspective greatly influenced U.S. sociology at the time, and it remains a source of inspiration. I can also say that *The Polish Peasant* was a reference for my colleagues and me when we were creating our own methodology for using life history in adult education.

Lewis's *The Children of Sanchez: Autobiography of a Mexican Family* (1961) also took a pioneering approach in the field of social science. Composed of the narratives of a father and his four children, it could be considered one of the first studies of a family group. The success of this anthropological work greatly influenced the comeback in the social sciences during the 1970s of qualitative methodologies such as biography. And the high level of the writing in this book also helped to popularize this approach. *The Children of Sanchez* has remained a counter-empirical model, pointing out the theoretical value of serious qualitative methods.

Immigration and also movement from rural to urban areas has been an object of research for decades. For example, life history has been used in a study at Laval University, in Quebec, centered on the cultural change of a generation of people who were eighteen to thirty years old in 1940. Society in Quebec was going through a profound transformation at the time, and the gap between the traditional rural areas and the growing cities was a source of conflict as the new generation sought its cultural identity. Life history was considered the right methodology for understanding people's life experiences and analyzing this problem. In France, Catani (1973), in his touching *Journal de Mohammed*, on the life of an Algerian worker, introduced the inner side of immigrants' lives and the difficulty, sometimes the sadness or the tragedy, endured by culturally displaced people. Catani was also very careful about sharing the credit for the writing with Mohammed. He refused to socialize Mohammed's testimony without mentioning Mohammed on the cover of the book, presenting him as coauthor.

These writings are typical products of the life history approach in social science. They do not address the field of education, but they have much to say to educators. In many countries the educational settings are becoming more and more multicultural, and educators, wherever they teach or work, must have a good level of knowledge in the social sciences in order to address ethnocentrism. In a way the biographical approach makes studies in the social sciences, such as Catani's book, easier for nonspecialists to appreciate.

Closer to adult education is the research by Wieslaw Theiss (1991) in Poland about the Polish children repatriated from Siberia and Manchuria from 1919 to 1923. As Theiss writes about his study of those he calls the Siberian Children, "the reconstruction of the life experiences of the Siberian Children would not have been possible without biographical studies" (p. 230). Theiss worked like a historian, considering his study an interactive learning process: "I treated the biographical method mainly as so-called social-activating study (active biography). Such a procedure is not limited to collecting autobiographical reports, but is a form of cooperative partnership in solving cognitive tasks. It is based on a dialogue and agreement. It is a way of learning not only about facts and events, but—what is sometimes even more significant—the meaning of particular events for the lives of particular persons" (p. 230).

Immigration, uprootedness, and identity are frequent topics for exploration in doctoral dissertations in human or social science. A few students are also dealing with such themes in the field of adult education, considering, from a biographical perspective, cultural or social changes as learning processes. For example, with financial support from the Swedish Council for Research in the Humanities and Social Sciences, Agnieska Bron-Wojciechowska started a project titled "Changes in an Adult's Life as a Reason for Learning: A Case of Polish Immigrants to Sweden." As she described it later (Bron-Wojciechowska, 1995), "the study concerned the changes in life situation of adults and their learning. I obtained several stories which portray very different personalities and different strategies which they choose to cope with changes" (p. 110).

The Relevance of Age

The theme of age introduces a series of social and human sciences themes that relate to adult education. The empirical approach to studying adults uses age not as a causal factor but as a category of analysis, showing needs or behaviors at various stages of adult life. Since the early studies done by Robert Havighurst (1953) and then by Bernice Neugarten (1964) and others on human development, life phases, and developmental tasks, age has always been considered a significant factor. The characteristics of adulthood have often been associated with specific chronological periods in a life cycle or life span, and researchers have frequently emphasized the characteristics of middle age. More recently, many publications have centered on adulthood and aging (Kimmel, 1980) or on old age and the last stages of life (Birren and Deutchman, 1991). A wide range of literature is now available that includes both data and speculative thinking about adulthood and its chronological life stages. Neugarten, for example has now published more than thirty books and articles in this area. Renée Houde (1986) presents a bibliography of about five hundred references on adult development, and the category of age appears frequently among them. Researchers are finding that even if they would prefer to avoid studying age, they have to take it into account (Levinson, 1978). Now, because of the "deinstitutionalization" of the life course, age tends to have another meaning. As Mark Tennant and Philip Pogson (1995) say, "the institutionalization of age, and the co-optation of society at large, makes it highly unlikely that individuals can chart alternative life courses, at least without considerable financial or personal cost.

There are forces moving against the continued institutionalization of the life course. Factors such as demographic and technological change, changes in male/female relations, and changes in the way work is organized do raise questions as to the extent to which society will continue to be age-graded in postmodern times" (p. 70).

In educational biographies, age is often mentioned even if it does not explain anything. Adults use age to tell something about themselves. In their narratives they often say in relation to age, "I still had time," or to the contrary, "It was too late." Adults have to deal with the meaning of their age many times during their lives. This work entails learning.

Changes in Roles and Status

Early publications in the field analyzed Buhler's idea of life goals and adults' changes in motivation during their lives (Kuhlen, 1970). Most later publications (reviewed for instance by Alan Knox, 1977) have concentrated on changes of status and role during the course of adult life. Adult education is necessary to help an individual to be a good parent, an active member of the community, or a creative user of leisure time. Experiencing the complexity of a meaningful marriage relationship, grieving over the loss of family members, and facing the necessity of renewing social life after some crisis are other examples of adult life difficulties that lead to learning experiences often mentioned in biographical narratives. In a similar literature review, Sharan Merriam (1984) identifies awareness of time, periods of introspection, societal influences, and the male-female role reversal that characterizes middle age as "learning opportunities for educational interventions." It is certainly relevant to associate adult education with the tasks and conflicts of adult life as long as the categories of analysis do not lead to a rigid model of adulthood or, as noted by Stephen Brookfield (1986), to the "conclusion that the typical adult learner is a relatively affluent, well-educated, white, middle-class individual" (p. 5). Less empirical studies, such as the one by Carol Gilligan (1982) on women's development, warn adult educators against hasty generalizations that would disregard the specific characteristics of adult life presented "in a different voice." The evolution of adults' conceptions of work has been seriously studied by Danielle Riverin-Simard (1984, 1993), with the intention of applying the research results to adult education. In his most recent book, Robert Kegan (1996) underlines beautifully how the mental demands of working and family life affect today's adult identity.

Life Stages Identified by Psychoanalysis and Humanist Psychology

The subtlety in Erik Erikson's presentation of the eight stages of man (1963) has certainly opened a path along which we can move out of the Freudian topology. Whether we call it culturalism or ego psychology, this enlargement was the first attempt since Jung's work to elaborate on adult development. Erikson's scheme has been frequently followed and even partly verified empirically. The idea that adult development is shaped in relation to a sequence of life conflicts organized around antagonistic polarities has had a strong influence in the field of adult education. The work of Roger Gould (1978) and Daniel Levinson (1978) should also be mentioned. Gould pointed out how adults are blocked in their development by unresolved conflicts from their earlier ages. Levinson created the helpful concepts of transitions, eras, and structure in life. Changes in adulthood require a five-year transition and necessitate transformation in complementary sectors of life such as family and work. Both Gould and Levinson are psychoanalysts; like Freud, they explain the dynamics of adult development through a clinical approach to studying a few individuals.

Jung's name does not appear very often in the literature on adult development. Levinson evokes Jung with the surprise of someone who did not intend to but had to read Jung's writings because of what he discovered in his own research. Jung, however, was the first psychologist to talk about adulthood and the midlife crisis. This silence about Jung is strange because his writing places him close to humanist psychology and to new age esotericism. In *The Adult Development of C. G. Jung*, John-Raphael Staude (1981) points out that Abraham Maslow's theory of self-actualization comes from Jung's ideas. Staude adds that Jung had an impact on the work of

Erich Fromm and Rollo May as well. For Staude, Jung's holistic research and interest in Tao was prophetic.

Phase Versus Stage of Development

The distinction between phase and stage of development, as underlined by K. Patricia Cross (1981, p. 174), is helpful because it points to two different but complementary dynamics. As Harry M. Lasker and James F. Moore (1979) write: "In the 'phasic' approach the aspects of development which are of interest are those which occur during relatively fixed chronological periods of adult life. By contrast, the 'stage' approaches focus on developmental changes in adulthood that are not well correlated with age" (p. 2). This statement accents the double temporality of adult development. Our social organization structures the phases of adult development into a kind of chronological socialization: school, work, marriage, parenthood, retirement, and in a parallel direction the life histories of adults show how the phases give adulthood its form. As some narratives show, an understanding of adult development requires an understanding of the specific interaction of phase and stage in the development of every adult. Adults have different rhythms, different reactions to their age, different ways to become aware of their social tasks. They do not all need adult education in the same way or at the same time in their lives, and because stages are more subtle and therefore more difficult to discover than phases, adult educators should consider how to identify specific stage changes in adulthood in each narrative as part of any educational work they accomplish with adults.

I would defend the idea, based on my own experience with educational biography, that learners often enter adult education as a means to dream and to deal with changes in the stages of adulthood. Adult education is an access, an escape, a transit, and a bypass as well as a failure or a success in the lives of adults. I also certainly consider how adults deal with their adulthood to be an essential part of their education as adults.

This view of double temporality puts the various theories of development in a more complementary perspective. Erikson and Levinson present life cycle phases that depend on a cultural or social structure of development, and Jean Piaget and Lawrence Kohlberg as well as James Loevinger (1976) emphasize stages that follow a sequential order of development. The work done by Elisabeth Kübler-Ross (1969) on the stages of accepting terminal disease illustrates well how the two temporalities may be combined. Individuals fall ill at a chronological phase of their lives, but their attitude toward death passes through stages such as denial, revolt, and depression that have nothing to do with that chronology but that relate to each patient's individual dynamics. By extension, as adults face unforeseen events, they go through a stage of disequilibrium that leads them to a new stability, and when they make decisions about the future, they are dealing more with a life phase. Change in adulthood can be seen either as a response to external events or as an internally motivated decision, and educational support might mean accompanying adults in their development in the present as well as preparing them for the future.

New Conditions for the Life Course

Many adults today are facing losses, mainly in the area of work but also in their family relationships. They have to adjust to ruptures that modify the structure and the meaning of their lives as adults. They have to painfully reshape their lives because they had not taken the time to think about how they would cope with unexpected stages in their personal development. The feeling of the jobless adult of being useless, for example, is stressed by Jean-Pierre Boutinet (1995), and Tennant and Pogson (1995) similarly remark that "economic, technological, and social change have an impact on life-course trajectories en masse, and often demand substantial psychological readjustment and the adoption of new discursive practices among those affected—with many casualties" (p. 112).

As young people have a different outlook from one generation to the next, the boundaries of adult life are also changing. The increasing aging of the population in Western societies is modifying society's image of adulthood. President Bush and President Clinton express not only two political choices but also two images of adulthood influenced by two periods of U.S. history. When they ask to be considered as adults, young people often also insist on the evolution of values and behaviors that are considered adult; conversely, they also resist becoming adult because it implies a respect for existing social norms they do not feel ready to demonstrate. The conflict between generations is in many ways a conflict between two representations of the dynamics of life. Erikson (1978) has been one of the few authors who stress the sociocultural meaning of the psychological stages of life. He argued that our present society has modified the timing of the passage from adolescence to adulthood, with many young people rejecting the idea of becoming adults.

Modern and Postmodern Adulthood

At a time when he was fighting National Socialism in Germany the theologian Dietrich Bonhoeffer, in his letters and notes written in prison before his execution, spoke about an adult faith. Were the German Christians who were following Hitler's dream of conquering the world counter-examples of adults, and was the decision to try to kill Hitler that Bonhoeffer had made more adult? Similar critical examples could be derived from our present time. Who are the adults in our troubled world? As adult educators we have an understanding of adulthood that is clearly related to our own hermeneutics of society. Adults analyze their biographies on the basis of the idea they have of adulthood.

More explicitly related to adult education is Mader's work on *guided autobiography*. Inspired by Birren and Deutchman (1991), Mader, a professor of adult education who is also a psychoanalyst, has created a "thematically guided autobiographical reconstruction"

that he has used with the aged, considering that "creating an acceptable autobiography is part of the continuous process of identity
building throughout life and up to death. . . . The autobiographical
reconstruction is used as a door into biographical analysis" (Mader,
1992, p. 244). Following Birren and Deutchman, Mader uses a *top-
ical approach* with nine steps: the story "of my important branching
points in my life, of my encounters with influential people, of my
handling of time, of my relationship to my body, money, learning,
food and drink, jobs and work and the development of my value orientation" (p. 248). "The main goal of Guided Autobiography in
adult education," concludes Mader, "is the creation of a true educational topic by the sequence itself. This sequence itself tries more
and more to work out the structural societal aspects [of a person's
biography] within the subjective individual dimension" (p. 256).

Women and Gender

Although in the social and human sciences literature some books
written by women employ a biographical style, not much in this
area has been written either by women or about women's life histories. There are many autobiographies written by men, but I found
no books dealing with men's culture based on biographical studies.

A few women who are sociologists have used the biographical
methodology. In the field of adult education, Bettina Daussien
(1995) recently published an important thesis in Germany addressing questions related to women's biography. In France a group of
feminists accustomed to the biographical methodology have written a book not yet published called "Being Author of Her Life," a
biographical construction of women's autonomy. Pineau's thesis
(Pineau and Marie-Michèle, 1983) addresses the theme of forming
a life through biography. In it, Pineau uses Marie-Michele's narrative to illustrate what education means in the process of building
one's own life.

Malika Belkaïd (1998) also gives an important place to the life
stories of women. Belkaïd's subjects are the first Algerian women to

be accepted for training in France at the Ecole Normale (teacher training college for primary school teachers). Several interviews with these women are analyzed, showing how a personal itinerary in a context of colonialism has to be understood as creating a cultural identity conflict.

Work, Unemployment, and Social Problems

Although authors are now addressing unemployment and the future of work, very few have looked at the effects of unemployment on the life history of the excluded. Socioeconomic analyses are more frequent than biographical testimonies of how unemployment affects the life course.

Gaulejac and Isabel Taboada Léonetti (1994) have assembled interviews of unemployed people in their book *La lutte des places* (The battle for a place). But the main contribution to this approach comes from Alheit's books and articles offering sociological analysis based on biographical studies. Stressing the socioeconomic conditions of our time, Alheit (1992) clearly indicates that people living in an unpredictable world can no longer use existing role models. In this uncertain world the traditional life's course, once accepted as a social institution and "organized around a working life biography, is becoming more and more diffuse" (p. 187). Owing to the instability of employment the structure of life has to take another form. The biographical road has been projected into the future.

As mentioned in Chapter Two, Alheit (1994) has explored unemployment among youths by conducting biographical interviews and analyzing the whole text of the interviews according to the methodology of grounded theory. His article on patchworkers (1995) studies biographical constructions and professional attitudes through an analysis of the new relation of young people, in this case students, to the new conditions of the world of work and employment. How do young people find their path as they have to face structural transformations of their biographies in today's world? Patchworking is described "as a biographical strategy for linking the continued promise of social ascent with the experience of actual exclusion" (p. 167).

Unemployed adult workers confronted with the same diffi-culties have used a type of biographical approach to share their experience in groups. Biographical techniques have also been de-veloped by social workers and adult educators who have worked with both unemployed workers and employees. But nothing spe-cific has come out of this work so far in terms of a systematic ap-proach or a publication.

In the context of counseling, Michel Legrand (1993) has written about his clinical work with alcoholics. His version of biography as an educational tool goes with his idea that alcoholics can benefit from reconstructing the meaning of their lives. Biography in this case is close to therapy. Other biographical studies have been published con-cerning work with adults who cannot read. Elisabeth Brugger (1995) mentions the importance of establishing the biographical background of adult illiterates attending basic training courses. Among the ques-tions raised are some directly concerned with educational biography: "Which life-events have occurred in their personal history? What kind of experience did they have at school? What attitude toward education has been passed on to them?" (p. 299).

Biography as Validation of Learning

The use of biography with adult reentry students brings us more specifically to the practice of biography in the field of adult educa-tion. Here, biography becomes an educational tool. Educational biography belongs to this category.

Biography might be used to validate experiential learning (Robin, 1992). However, the success of this approach will vary with the group. With some colleagues, I have used biography in the context of continuing education with students at levels of for-mal education below the university level. It has been extremely difficult to go deeper than the description of some previous school experiences. At these levels, adult students are afraid to go back to their life histories. They might feel ashamed of their pasts or have painful memories they do not want to revisit. In contrast, preparing educational biographies at the university level gives students the opportunity to deal with many aspects of the past, whatever they might be: family, school, friendship, and so forth. In the university context the biographical approach clarifies adults' relation to knowledge (Dominicé and others, 1999).

Linden West (1996) describes the same kind of experience: preparing a biography is a help to reentry adult students who have doubts about their capacity to learn. Some students at the University of Geneva have clearly shown that school learning recovers its meaning in the light of life experiences. In other words, life experiences may allow adults to credit what they learned at school. Many higher education external degree programs have staff in adviser roles, sometimes referred to as counselor-tutors or mentors. They help adult participants with the process of setting educational goals, selecting activities, and assessing progress. They may also locate learning resources for students, such as library materials, people with specific expertise, and computer databases. They may give them a way to reflect on connections between learning and their family, work, and hobbies. These advisers, through such means as coaching, study sessions, and workshops, can help participants use journals, life histories, and other forms of educational biography to clarify their preferred learning styles, select educational resources, recognize situational influences, and chart educational and career directions. The resulting insights can also help them reflect on past learning related to their adult roles and recognize the strengths and directions this learning can bring to their studies.

Social Factors in Higher Education Experiences

The purpose of another study was to find out how societal dynamics were reflected in the higher education experiences of a particular group of returning students. Juanita Johnson-Bailey and Ronald M. Cervero (1996) report on an analysis of educational biographies of black women who began their higher education after age thirty. Interviews were used to obtain the educational biographies, which were then analyzed (see Bogdan and Biklen, 1982; Casey, 1994; Denzin, 1989, for discussions of this kind of analysis). Open-ended questions explored the women's most pleasant and unpleasant memories of school and the resulting stories centered on cultural concerns. These narratives were tape-recorded, transcribed, and analyzed as text. The written analyses included extensive quotations related to the emerging themes. In describing how they dealt with academia, these returning students referred to strategies that included silence, negotiation, and resistance.

The educational biographies of the black women in this study did not reflect the motives reported from earlier studies of majority reentry women, which emphasized self-fulfillment for displaced homemakers, a response to the empty-nest syndrome, or further advancement for career women (Peck, 1986). Further, school enrollment for majority women was affected by family background, marriage, children, and previous success in school. In contrast, these black women stated that they were returning to school in hope of a better job and a better life, even though they realized that their advancement in school would be affected by race and gender, which had influenced and would continue to influence their lives. They decided to enter higher education regardless of past school failures, lack of family support, and child-care concerns. They observed that the strongest deterrents to their participation in any schooling were their classroom and social encounters with racism and gender subordination, in which they felt excluded, devalued, isolated, and viewed as less than capable. They understood that the societal forces that shaped their lives were also present in the classroom, which was a microcosm of the larger society.

Continuing Professional Education

Traditionally, most of the learning professionals do throughout their careers has been self-directed (Houle, 1980). However, increased specialization and use of educational technology is increasing the amount of this continuing professional education that is practitioner directed, experience based, and organized around practice problems and context. Penny A. Jennett and Thomas G. Pearson (1992) report that such workplace learning can reduce barriers related to being away from the practice and can increase the likelihood that learning will be applied. An educational biography approach can help professionals learn how to learn more effectively by reflecting on their process and results when they learned well in the past. Such practice-based learning combines attention to professional, social, personal, and situational influences and benefits and promotes interaction with peers and experts that can also contribute to improved performance.

To benefit from such practice-based learning, professionals must cultivate attitudes and procedures that enable them to assume responsibility for their learning. For example, they can identify opportunities for improvement with practice profiles, self-assess educational needs, set priorities for learning activities, use educational technology, include associates when making changes, use learning contracts, and evaluate their learning activities and outcomes. For health care workers, discussing clinical cases with other members of the health care team is an especially beneficial educational biography approach to improving health care and advancing one's career. As professionals make explicit the assumptions, influences, plans, activities, and results of their past learning, they can become more reflective practitioners and acquire better guides to their future learning.

Biography in the Training of Adult Educators

Several biographical methods have been used in the preparation of adult educators at the University of Geneva and later at the University of Paris-Dauphine, the Catholic University of Louvain-la-Neuve, and Columbia University's Teachers College in New York City. My own practice with educational biography began and has developed within the context of my teaching at the University of Geneva. Basically, the idea is for adult educators to analyze their educational biographies in order to better understand the processes of learning that characterize the adults with whom they work. I would say that this course's content gives educational biography its greatest impact. This is because the reflection about the processes of learning occurs during a process of learning and at the place where learning is supposed to be the most meaningful, namely the university. With adult educators I strongly emphasize, as I mention in a previous chapter, the difference between educational biography and a biographical approach. Educators, if they want to understand the biographical impact of adult learning, must go through the whole group process of preparing oral and written narratives, discussing each version, and analyzing the written version. The program offered by the University of Geneva Office of Continuing Education for educators who cannot take the regular course requires ten full days, with two three-day periods of residence.

Time is an important vehicle of learning. As I wrote in a recent article (Dominicé, 1996), research takes more time than training. One thing the process of educational biography does not help adult students to do is to find the right distance from biography so they can work as researchers themselves. To become researchers, they would need a second phase, as my seminar students get when they prolong their educational biography through a paper or a dissertation.

Some Additional Uses of Educational Biography

Life history approaches are becoming increasingly familiar in adult and continuing education in the United States. Religious educators are videotaping oral history sessions to enable prominent congregation members to share with members of their religious community both influences and insights related to their spiritual journeys. Secondary and higher education teachers from humanities and social sciences are inviting elders to share their firsthand stories for intergenerational discussion. Retirement and elder care staff members are arranging for older adults to write about and discuss their reminiscences for the benefit of all concerned. In each instance a major theme is learning, and sharing written, oral, or videotaped life stories helps all concerned reflect on the process.

For example, *Life Stories in Library Programming* is a video-based course prepared by Marsha Rossiter and Darlene E. Weingand (1996). The authors argue that life histories are valuable in library programs because they contain rich material for learning by adults of all ages. They can become powerful metaphors, helping people make sense of their lives and share that understanding with others. The learning that results is associated with adult development. Young adults attend to their search for identity, changing interpersonal relations and values and acquiring self-confidence. Older adults engage in life review. Narrative memories help people recall events and understand their deeper symbolism, which also reveals and creates meaning. Sharing life histories creates a shared world and a sense of continuity over time among people.

The authenticity of contemporary stories makes them especially powerful. For example, in *Corporate Legends and Lore*, Peg Neuhauser (1993) concludes that in the workplace, information from personal experience is more believable than information transmitted by other means. Sharing stories with others is personal, immediate, and dynamic. Interaction contributes empathic understanding and builds community. Although each life history is unique, each also reflects a cultural context that is the context of other people's lives as well. Major themes in such stories are interpersonal relations, transitions, and psychological changes. Sharing such remembrances is helpful to others facing similar situations (Kaufman, 1968; Keen and Valley-Fox, 1989).

People who help adults learn in any settings, such as libraries, retirement arrangements, religious institutions, community agencies, or educational institutions, can assist them to address the learning theme. As adults do so, it is important that they reflect on topics important to them, in ways that enrich their search for meaning and self-direction, as they also consider situational influences. Sometimes it is helpful to encourage them to consider special events, local history, occupational experiences, adventures, conflicts, and peak experiences. As people are telling their stories, they can be encouraged to give attention to listener interest, and to story themes, setting, characters, and events.

Finally, educational biography can also be a valuable adjunct to the field-based experiential learning associated with some adult and continuing education. An example of such learning is coming to recognize how people learn to care about the environment, as reflected in individuals' own support for conservation, recycling, reduction of pollution, and contributions to sustainable practices. As people reflect on and share their stories about such environmental issues, they can deepen their understanding and commitment. Such use of educational biography can also help them engage in knowing in action and in discovering emerging issues and directions for their learning in the future (Jackson and Caffarella, 1994; Merriam, 1993; Schön, 1987).

Some Issues for Future Research and Analysis

Clearly, we can investigate further the diverse biographical traditions that lie behind educational biography, and we can continue to build a literature that analyzes and reports on the many ways educational biography can be used in practice. But the present discussion also suggests some general issues that we particularly need to continue discussing and analyzing. We need to talk more about ethics and also about methodology, especially as it involves incorporating research into training.

Ethics

In Chapter Two, I discussed the ethical issue of quoting from others' narratives in research. Some educators and researchers refuse to quote extracts from biographical texts in their articles and books. Others believe it is an acceptable practice as long as they ask the students for permission. The members of ASIHVIF have a rule about this problem that everyone respects. We consider it unethical to use biographical material without consulting the author of the narrative.

However, this principle does not seem to be shared by most sociologists, who quote what they hear with the precaution only of disguising names and social identities. Catani seems to be an exception. His position might be explained by the fact that he focuses on one person's life story at a time (Catani and Mazé, 1982). In this approach the relationship between the researcher and the person whose story is to be told takes a lot of space and time to build up before the narrative can be constructed. The ethical dimension is fairly discussed by Catani, focusing on the central question of who is the "first author," as Catani says.

Ferrarotti (1983), speaking about biographical narratives, talks about the personal testimonies that he feels honored to be allowed to listen to. He indicates that sociologists must be respectful of the confidences they receive. A biographical approach may be taken as a commitment. The practice of biography as a methodology of research in social science is therefore not easy. Indeed, as Rudolf Egger (1995), an Austrian professor and member of the ESREA network, has shown, asking for a life history narrative may make the researcher feel like a spy. He offers this example:

Sabine and Gertrud have been participants in a research-seminar using biographical methods. After acquiring a theoretical basis in interpretative analysis and the sociology of deviant groups in society, they decided to explore the processes of becoming a member in a group of homeless. They looked for "empirical material" and it was easy to locate a group of homeless who they then contacted. After initial talks in the street they tried to make a narrative interview, but from that time on there was a growing feeling of apprehension on both sides. Later they told me they felt like spies, like policemen, like question-machines which wanted to change human beings into spoken material.

Ethical questions are central to the practice of adult education. Biographical work has the potential to become more instrumental and to end up as a parody of the learning process. A kit has been published in France, for example, that offers a kind of guided biographical approach in which the person using the kit offers answers or solutions to a set series of biographical questions. This could promote versions of biographies that adults can produce quickly but that may not be as useful for analysis and reflection as narratives that are authentically the authors' in all respects.

Methodology

In several parts of this book, I address myself to methodological questions. Such questions seem unending, and we need more investigation of them. If we take biography as a general field of research, then one important methodological issue is defining the kinds of materials we identify as biography. For instance, are oral and written narratives complementary? What kinds of written narratives might be expected when the authors are not students in an academic setting? Oral approaches are often used when the people presenting their stories have low educational levels. What are the minimum conditions a life story must meet to become a biography? Or to put it another way: on what basis can an oral interview or a written text about personal experiences be taken as biography?

The purpose of educational biography is to transform biography into a learning process. Combining learning and research as educational biographies do is an ambitious objective. From the point of view of conducting research, does learning by the author have to be a part of educational biography? If such learning *is* part of what needs to happen to make research by both the author and the external researcher efficient, it clearly means that we need to rethink adult education research that does not attend to the learning process.

Thinking about methodology also requires us to think about epistemology. Whatever form a biography takes, it is always an interpretation. People speak about themselves; people write about themselves; people answer questions about themselves. Basically, they socialize the life story they have been telling to themselves by telling it to others. This world of interpretation is often dependent on the dialogue that takes place with a researcher, and this social situation certainly influences the content of the narratives. The researcher might be a teacher, a member of the clergy, or a doctor. The answers to the researcher's questions will be different according to the image the participant projects onto the researcher, given the researcher's profession. What should researchers do about their influence? Is educational biography an answer to the problem of influence?

When I read the written version of an educational biography, I realize the extent to which the oral narrative has been a first phase for maturing the life story told. At the same time, I often ask myself if I should not have questioned the author more during the oral version in order to further provoke this maturation. The dividing line between being too nondirective and being too directive is again debatable. Should we as researchers take an interpretation as it comes, or in the interests of the object of research, should we help adults be more consistent by helping them construct their narratives? Is guided autobiography a good example? Should we consider guided educational biography? This problem is related to what I call the *level of consciousness* of the participants. The researcher might help the participant by asking "the right question," a question that is the participant's own existential question.

Across the variety of biographical approaches the methodological questions appear to remain the same. At the same time, the practice of biography brings the opportunity to explore new ways to do research. In the domain of adult education, we need to become creative on the matter of research because adult educators often work well yet seldom reflect on their action. This lack of reflection can affect biographical work if it takes place in pieces in different programs and little effort is made to formalize the result. Even though educational biography can put research into action, the use of biography in adult education is too often a missed opportunity for research.

Summary

The biographical approach belongs to a recent trend that has revitalized life history as a research methodology in social science. Educational biography is a version of life history applied to the field of adult education. It has been developed, along with other biographical approaches, in the context of two European networks, one primarily French speaking and the other multicultural.

Life history has long been practiced in Western civilization. The more recent work can be categorized by three types of research and several dominant themes. Both categories of analysis can help us understand the specificity of educational biography. Themes such as immigration, women's issues, and unemployment show how much the methodology of life history relates to social issues.

In the field of adult education, biographical approaches have been used for the training of adult educators and as tools for guiding adult students and fostering their process of self-directed learning. Shorter approaches to educational biography serve the same purpose as longer ones even though they result in less depth.

Finally, the practice of biography in educational settings raises some key ethical issues and unending questions about the relationship between researchers' purposes and learners' purposes as they work with educational biographies. We need to recognize these matters and develop a more extensive discussion of them in the educational biography literature.

Chapter Four

How Adults Educate Themselves

The process of educational biography results in narratives. This chapter offers excerpts from some narratives that illustrate some of the themes that have emerged from my research. These themes, summarized at the end of the chapter, reflect the types of content likely to emerge from educational biographies in any adult and continuing education effort.

Adult students are not generally asked to discuss adulthood in their narratives. However, preparing their educational biographies is a learning process that gives meaning to aspects of their adulthood. This process is sometimes more important than the result. Their struggle for the independence to become themselves is a central factor in adults' interpretation of their life histories. "Being adult means being autonomous," writes one participant, who adds, "There is not a right age to reach this autonomy of adulthood. It depends so much on factors such as family, school, and life and on how we find peace within these dimensions." In this chapter I explain, through the different testimonies that I quote, the processes through which adults educate themselves to become more autonomous. I also explore how they interpret these processes.

For most adults, thinking about their education calls up a strong memory of being dependent during their childhood on the presence, love, authority, and decisions of their parents. The first learning experience of life has to do with accepting, to a greater or lesser extent, being educated by others. Adulthood is then interpreted as the counter-experience of building one's own life, without being told where to go and what to do. Family, school, and community are the three contexts that adults identify when they describe the process through which they gained autonomy. The rebellious time of adolescence is sometimes mentioned, but the passage between dependency and autonomy is more complex than the passage through one stage of life. Many adults are aware of feeling an ambivalence about childhood and adulthood. The process of becoming autonomous does not mean the end of this ambivalence, but it does usually mean becoming more at peace with the two. Educational biography helps adults realize how their self-concepts have been shaped by other people.

In and out of the Family

Most adults have detailed understandings of their relationships with each of their parents. They interpret their attitudes toward schooling, occupational choice, and marriage through the lenses of their immediate family experience. They felt closer to one parent or admired one more than the other. As children, they knew that at least one parent would disapprove of their decisions concerning, for example, school or friendship. Sometimes they had no choice but to study for the certificate their parents wanted them to acquire. Sometimes they agreed to receive training for the job their parents thought was good for them before they had taken time to think about the job they really wanted. This was not only a matter of acceding to authority. One student wrote: "I remember when I was ten years old my parents, who were both working in a hotel, telling me: we do not want you to experience in your life what we had to go through; we want you to have an easier life which means that you have to study; we will give you the opportunity to study as much as you want."

Parents act for the well-being of their children, and it sometimes takes years before adults feel that they are entitled to their own opinions and, if necessary, to disagree with their parents. After twenty years of rebellion against his father and his family circle, which he described as an "iron collar," and after having had many experiences as a primary school teacher, as a monk, and a member of an underground group involved with political refugees, a man over thirty wrote in his narrative: "Coming back to my home town, I learned to look at each member of my family, especially my father, for himself and without looking for agreement; it is not always easy. After absorbing my family's values and later rejecting them, I experienced my return as an important step toward the values of my education." Sometimes the feeling of being imprisoned is so strong that there is a deep need to walk out: "Two months after turning twenty, my coming of age, I left my family without anything, no clothes, no money. I had been suffocating and decided to 'rescue' myself by moving thousands of miles away. I did not know anything about working or making money. Being European but living in North Africa, I had never crossed a road by myself. I started a new life, my first step toward adulthood." This breaking through has been dreamt of and also experienced by many women, who sometimes admit in their narratives to having used their relationship with a man and marriage as an excuse to leave. Many adults who did not rebel when they were young tell of going through a conflictual relationship later in their lives.

The road to adulthood seems to go through stages of standing up to one's family; only after that does it becomes possible to accept one's parents for who they are. Women sometimes emphasize the work they had to do to improve their relationship with their mothers. One woman wrote that "the search for autonomy from my mother has been the dominant thought of my entire life. When I was two years old I wanted to stand up to my mother's will and this revolt lasted all my childhood, teens, and until I was married." And she added, "The choice to become a nurse was one of my first victories." After this period of rebellion, she went through two more stages in the process of gaining autonomy: a stage of negotiation through all kinds of discussions and a stage of listening. She was helped in the second stage by being married and financially independent, but still, she says, "I felt it was necessary to explain to my mother and to prove how different I was. I needed her to understand me and to agree with me at least once." The need to rebel and the need to be recognized form a paradox that many adults face.

The absence of parents does not simplify this process: the rebellion takes other forms, and the suffering may be deeper. In some narratives, participants confessed that they did not feel they had to revolt against their parents. One man wrote: "From an early age, my parents made me responsible by telling me: 'You do what you want, what you consider the best for yourself because we trust you and you seem responsible,'" and he added: "This is why I never had any adolescence, in the traditional sense of the term, in my life history." For me this is a good example that the struggle for autonomy, which characterizes the process of growing up, does not necessarily imply psychological conflict with parents.

Several other family members, such as grandparents, brothers, or sisters, were mentioned when they acted as parent substitutes, a situation that often led to a similar need for distance. The place an individual occupied as a child in the family group had a strong influence. Karen analyzed the educative role played by her older sister: "The admiration for my first-born sister, the pride of taking part in her life, the memory of being manipulated and exploited, the wish to do better than her, forced me to take central decisions for my life such as vocational choice as reaction or even revenge. I needed to explode and find my way out of her misuses of authority."

Adults have many ways of educating themselves. There is no definitive model of autonomy. The narratives offer different interpretations of an unending inner debate between conformity and autonomy, which is a key challenge of education. Depending on the life phase or the context of the moment, there are various forms of the need to "come back home" and check family roots and of the need "to take off in a more creative expression of oneself."

For younger students today the instability of the economic context seems to influence the tension they feel between conformity and autonomy. The new generation does not have to free itself from a heritage of doctrinairism as much as to find the right references for the difficult choices to be made. Whereas older adult students were mainly driven by the need to emancipate themselves, the new generation is, first of all, preoccupied by possessing a place in society and finding a way to survive.

Finding Room for Oneself in the School Environment

The same basic conflict was present in the biographies on the topic of schooling. Whereas some adults described their school years as a continuous burden, others considered schooling a key part of the process of educating themselves. Some students had to stop their schooling because of their parents' insistence that they enter vocational training or professional life or because they had bad grades and could not continue. Many of these adults were pleased to be able to go back to school. When they received their admission to the university, many were scared but nevertheless happy to have an opportunity to achieve what they were unable to do earlier in their lives. They expressed the idea of "repairing their past." As a nurse explained: "After failing at [secondary] school when I was in the last year, I thought I could heal my pain by going to the university." Another adult wrote something similar: "I consider the university . . . a revenge against the bad conditions of my school years." The emancipatory process of becoming oneself seems to depend on following some kind of traditional education. In more general terms, the construction of the learning process can be identified more with the process of socialization toward adulthood than with the building of a body of knowledge acquired through learning the content of the different subjects present in the curriculum.

There is also a dialectic between family and school, a mutual reinforcement. According to their narratives some adults felt socially uncomfortable during some phase of their school years because of their family background. As an adult student named Peter said: "The sociocultural differences strongly influenced the general atmosphere of the class. As the son of a grocer, I felt isolated among future lawyers, doctors, and notaries. Today I realize that the desire to prove to myself that I was as able as the others made me decide to continue." Others, like this young woman, used school to stress their distance from their family: "No one had studied on both sides of my family, and no one seemed to have regretted it, because for members of my immediate family study belonged to another world. The will to remove myself from this family model is the real reason for my good grades."

Adults almost always remembered the teachers who did not necessarily follow the rules or who chose topics according to their own taste and often passion, even if those topics were outside the program. They also recalled unpleasant teachers, those who gave bad grades, scared their students, and sometimes even hit them. This memory is painful for those adults who consider their teachers responsible for their failure, like the student who recalled that "my difficulties at school were made worse by the destructive attitude of one of my teachers, who forced me to drop school and start an apprenticeship."

Being part of a group of students can bring out good memories, including memories of having fun breaking the rules with peers. Adults educate themselves through attempts to challenge the rules rather than to follow them. One participant, a woman in charge of teacher training programs, recognized in her narrative that "I have a real but unclear impression that I have not been, during my school years, the author of my education, but on the contrary have been educated according to the desires of my teachers and have acquired knowledge which does not result from my own process of learning." This confession stresses the view that the process of having one's own ideas includes a kind of opposition to the official knowledge received from a teacher. For some participants the difficulty of identifying with their peers troubled the course of their high school years. For many, being good at school created conflicts in their process of socialization, because being good at school meant following the school's path, but to become adults they felt they had to invent their own path into an unknown world. As one narrative said: "It was only when I could verify that I was adequate to this learning context that I could begin to take my training seriously."

For young people, as much as for adults, school and adult education have their own agendas.

The Cultural Context of Education

Our sociocultural environment is another significant influence on our adulthood. Every adult is raised in a value system he or she is expected to express. According to their educational biographies, many adults find religion is central to their education. As one student said: "We were very surprised to discover the importance of religion in our lives, its astonishing impact in spite of the variety of meanings possible." Religion has been for many students the source of their radical political commitment, although their need to be autonomous made some reject the religion associated with their education. In many narratives the will to serve other people, the poor or the sick, or a high expectation for the social or political relevance of a vocational choice appears to be the direct result of the students' religious background. The narratives often express individuals' search for a spirituality to claim once they have abandoned, as one woman said, "the rubbish which has been inculcated in them."

In a time of cultural turmoil it is not easy to know what values adults finally recognize as their own. Adults need to be recognized and accepted by the people they feel close to, but at the same time they need to make decisions that express their own identities. For most adults their dominant values remain those inherent in the cultural models of roles they have internalized in the course of their education: "It was when I became a mother and when I held my infant daughter that I had the true impression of entering into the world of adulthood." One woman in her forties expressed very clearly the conflict she felt between the values of her education and more modern values: "I think I am a mother and a professional. The ancestral values handed down to me by my mother are alive in me and guide me; but the need to be active socially and to develop personally worries me. These last years I have been totally busy with the strain of finding a more or less harmonious coexistence between these values in me."

For men, a similar conflict is sometimes mentioned in relation to the value of work and its place in their lives when they realize what they must renounce for their careers. After analyzing the narratives, I found that there is a correlation between the values dominating the men's culture and their attitude toward schooling. The principal sociocultural mode for men is professional. As one group recognized in its communal work of analysis, school is the first step toward professional integration. In doing their homework, men believe that they are already on their way to a job. And the values of traditional male work shape their vocational itineraries. As they explain it in their narratives, men who have initially chosen to be social workers or psychologists have such a difficult time being accepted in the traditional social environment outside their work that they sometimes choose another profession.

Sociocultural closeness, sometimes along with the phenomenon of exclusion, is mentioned by adults from rural areas. It is related to the difficulties of adaptation they experienced when moving to another cultural environment. However, traveling to another country can allow an individual to gain the distance needed to work on his or her identity. One student reported: "I took time to form the idea of leaving and going to live in North Africa. This break was due to many different reasons: family, social, and professional life; culture; religion; climate. . . . I never felt as much myself as during these years. . . . For the first time I was free to think, to be without family or social obligations. . . . The will to adapt in the encounter with people was so different from the one I had known before being forced to define myself far from unacceptable constraints."

From Detachment to Self-Affirmation

Adults build their lives with the materials given them by their education. Adulthood can be understood as the process of transforming this heritage into a personal form. The educational biography approach offers the adult an interpretation of his or her never-ending struggle for identity. The difficult process of becoming oneself implies confronting, in one's life project and learning experiences, the values and models acquired from family, school, and social life. Adults' reflections about these three dominant contexts show a kind of ambivalence between two conflicting goals: the desire for detachment from the emotional, cultural, and social ties of childhood and youth and the need to keep in touch with one's roots. The distance from the past that an adult achieves, contributes to a kind of self-confidence that I have heard expressed orally as well as in written narratives. This self-confidence tends to be expressed in relation to work and to knowledge.

The following short review of five educational biographies offer an idea of the process through which adults have become themselves through their education. The authors of the first three narratives are struggling with the meaningfulness of their working life. Alan is an adult educator telling about the construction of his professional identity. Lucy is a woman who is trying to stay alive and be creative. Paul followed various steps to finally achieve what he wanted as his profession. They are all in their late thirties or early forties.

During his entire professional life to date, Alan has been looking for "something which agrees with me without knowing exactly what." At the end of high school, his choice was not clear. He finally became an engineer but "was not too sure" of this career path. So, he said, "I chose general mechanics because it would give me a larger choice." After his military duty, he decided not to go back to school and applied for a job in a multinational corporation. Four years later, looking for a different lifestyle and thinking about business school, he made the decision to stop working for a while and think about his future, but he underlined that he "did not want to move irreparably off the track." He then went back to work for the same corporation and says of his job, "I am trying to work in a way which suits my personality." He is still, ten years later, looking for something closer to his goals but admits that he does not know what. He wants to be more involved with people in his job, and because he had some practice as an adult instructor in his field, he decided to take the risk of leaving his job to become an associate partner in a small consulting company running continuing education programs. Later he decided to become a freelance adult educator and consultant. He interprets his professional change this way: "My responsibility in different companies has made it clear to me that, in the long run, it is not worth it to betray yourself; work has to agree with your person. I wanted to reduce the distance between my job and my deep being. Becoming an adult educator seems to give me the opportunity to develop through my job."

Lucy was centered on what happened in her inner self: "I wanted to earn my own money in order to be autonomous from a stuffy family. This is why, after a short period of study, I became a bookkeeper in a bank. I had been raised with the value that work was a central part of life." At the time of the narrative she had spent ten years in the same bank and was refusing the passive model most of her colleagues adopted. She wrote: "I want to have a more interesting job and I have learned that in order to face reality, one must be constantly active. . . . For two years I worked hard because I wanted to prove that it was possible for a woman to succeed in a world of men." She then asked to go to London to improve her English, and she took advantage of this time alone to enjoy herself and meditate about her future. She realized that she needed more time to think, and she asked to reduce her time at work. She began to take courses at the university, and in her narrative she says: "In order to find my identity, I have tried to challenge myself from different perspectives. Conflicts, changes, and questioning in life are part of the dynamics of the learning process."

Paul had several jobs before he finally decided to become a yoga teacher. His first job was as a sheet metal worker, and then he worked in a bakery before starting his apprenticeship to be a technician specializing in precision mechanics. After some years he decided to take night classes in order to become an engineer. After obtaining his diploma he worked as an engineer in a number of companies. However, after being introduced to yoga by a friend and studying psychology at the university, with complementary work in psychoanalysis and "sophrology" (loosely, self-control), he made the decision to became a yoga teacher. Whatever change such a choice meant in terms of budget or family life, Paul is progressing personally, asserting what he feels is the central part of himself.

The individual's search for a personal meaning in working life is a widespread theme in the biographies. When adults confront new choices, these choices often include improvement in their intellectual life. As a child educator wrote in his narrative about his continuing education: "I must now read, write and think much more than ever before. I consider this task to be, for me, an opening to a more adult stage of development." The two extracts I quote from next both deal with this emancipatory dimension of thinking. Betty is a women who struggled to build a meaningful aspect to personal thinking. Johnny expressed doubts about his capacities.

Betty came from a working-class background and, because she did not have the money to study beyond high school, used her commercial certificate to work as a secretary for some years before she decided to ask for a loan and go to a school for social workers. She shared numerous memories from her childhood about learning at school, saying, "I felt great at school and I loved to learn, to read," and repeating later, "The teachers were strict but I loved to learn." Outside school she had other learning experiences; she learned music and sports and often went to public libraries. Church was also a place for learning. She wrote that it offered "groups and Bible, two worlds to explore, to understand. I felt again the need to go further and to know more." But it was only in her training as a social worker that she discovered the way to transform external knowledge into personal knowledge by relating professional competence to personal development. She says: "One must connect knowledge and being. One must learn to say no, to find oneself, to find one's way alone. Is that becoming adult?" She wanted to know more and more; she had a strong feeling about her lack of knowledge.

She raised four children, and when the last one was nine months old, she wanted to work half time and study psychology at the university. She feared the masculine models of knowledge but wanted to discover "new tools to construct her own way of think-ing, a way to reflect which was hers." "Should I not try," she says, "to be equipped to understand the motherly silence . . . and also the motherly language? We have to create our worlds, by questioning more than by being affirmative, by reasoning with resonance. Our language has to be an expression of our total person, an expression of breaking through as well as our inner reconciliation, symbolic and real journeys between a father who knows and a mother who feels, interpersonal knowledge produced by emerging new relationships."

Writing about the time he spent at the university as an adult, Johnny said that "the first year gave me the opportunity to check the level of my capacities. I felt I had been touching the walls be-fore coming in. It was when I felt adequate to the context that I could first be involved in my learning process. I then decided to enlarge the knowledge used in my daily existence and to think about a professional identity which was defined without being only the opposite of the identity of others."

This close relationship between knowledge and identity is not relevant only for university students. Being empowered in their way of thinking, in sharing ideas, in imagining alternative types of life is for adults a releasing process. Adult educators working in the field of personal expression or development are fully aware of this. The structure and style of educational biographies are centered on this process of helping adults assert themselves, of empowering adults throughout their lives. This is a priority of adult education.

The adults I have quoted are not heroes or models. They are average adults with university backgrounds who are looking for ways to become themselves. Their learning processes are at the center of their educational biographies and indicate the parts of their lives that have been directly associated with learning. Methodological questions about the validity of the theoretical contribution offered by biographical narratives remain open. I believe that each educa-tional biography as it is told in a narrative is the expression of a sin-gular life history as well as a reflection of a more general learning process. Because quantitative data are not a necessary condition of validity for me, many biographies, resulting from years of research, contribute to my relevant hypotheses. The knowledge required by educators finds its meaning in the context of action. Theory should help the reflection of practitioners. Here we are not in the world of empirical data conducive to prescriptive knowledge. The idea of a knowledge made mainly out of relevant hypotheses gives educational biography its validity as a methodology of research in the field of education.

Alice's Dynamics of Education and Her Process of Learning

As a last and more complete example, I offer a extensive summary of the biographical narrative of an adult student named Alice.

From her childhood in a small village in the Alps come "some fugitive images": "a life outdoors, submitting to the rhythm of games, gardening, and worship." Her mother "comes from a rural social class." Her father joined her "mother's village to work as the primary school teacher." Her family is "very Catholic and deeply conservative." Moreover, she adds, "My childhood takes place in a world dominated by women. . . . The strong individuality of the women in my family contrasted with a more hidden role played by the men. . . . This was stressed more in the case of my father because of his absence a good part of the year, since he was paid only during the months the school was open." She concludes that "my identity was built outside the world of men, and meeting this world later in life was not without difficulties." She underlines this theme because, as she says: "At school, boys and girls did not attend the same classes . . . furthermore, the girls were with Catholic nuns, the boys with the primary school teacher."

Alice's school years were profoundly affected by this environment. "Memory of my entire school attendance," she wrote, "is imprinted by religious influence, the worst one, the one based on fear. And my family will not let me escape. As a little girl I am taken, I fall into the trap: my dreams as a child are full of devils. I swallow, almost greedily, all the moral values and convictions."

The fundamental influence of religious education, of the collusion between school and religion entertained by her family, is something Alice will have to accept until the end of high school, which she attends first "in a religious school run by sisters" in a small town, then in a school of the Ursulines in the main city of the county where she graduated. "My teenage years," she says, "can be defined with two words: activism and mysticism. Outside class, where I did not have any problems, I committed myself to different groups mainly characterized by religious influence. When I believed that I was called by God, twice I spent a period of time in a monastery." She specifies that owing to this experience, "the world of men is still totally strange for me; I do not look at boys; I have great difficulty accepting my femininity." In addition, "There remains one flaw in this edifice of my life: mixed with students from other social classes, I began to feel a kind of alliance between religion and the upper class."

Some months later she arrives in a university located in a small town. She begins to take time for herself, spending more time "enjoying myself than studying." According to her own expression, "a slow process of doubt is starting in myself," reinforced by one of her teachers who is a convinced radical. "It is shaking many of my certitudes and points of reference," she writes; "My opposition to religion is becoming violent." She adds, "like Mr. Seguin's goat, I rush blindly. I begin an open conflict with my own family. To confront them is a strong move for me and it will take a lot of time later to recuperate from this." From this time on, Alice became a political militant as well as a fully involved feminist. She first becomes active on a committee for Chile and "gets used to the leftist jargon," although confessing, "I feel bare of my religious clothing and the disapproval of my family weighs heavily on me." A little later she would recognize, however, that "what is important for me is my political commitment. I am also discovering feminism, the emerging movement of women's groups. The fascination of the first meetings, the joy of the discovery of sisterhood."

Then "one day I free myself from everything. . . . I have most of my former companions against me when I tell them suddenly that the Church and a revolutionary Marxist group are the same: the same need for certitudes, for a line of behavior directed from above." This new need for breaking loose led her to a new university environment. She moved to a bigger city. About this choice, she says, "I decided to slow down the tendency to escape what I was living for years. It is really time for me to seriously start to study or work cognitively." She admits that her "previous study had been a pretext to do something totally different," even though she recognizes that she had learned how to work. Alice invested a lot of energy into this second stage of university study, working especially on the problem of women's education, because she considers this theme fundamental for understanding the years she has just spent.

Looking at these recent years as a whole, she states:

What I could call my life journey and its cohesiveness is slowly becoming visible. Eighteen years were almost completely spent on building myself according to the way expected of me, for gulping down the culture of my environment. Because I am passionate, I bought it all. I am not then surprised that the opposition was so violent and needed many stages. . . . I have a clear feeling that the phase of major turmoil has finished. . . . I feel that I got rid of most of the sociocultural shell which prevented me from reaching my own self, from discovering my deepest wishes. I like to compare myself to a house whose stones fell down, which was rebuilt, and continues to be maintained; however, my foundation remains solid. This foundation is an ever-present strength, a kind of self-confidence given to me, perhaps through the admiration that my parents always gave me, a hunger to go on and to understand.

She adds to this, as she has just tragically lost a twenty-year-old cousin, "New questions are emerging. . . . Because of the mourning, which has shown suffering but not revolt by my family, I have a new openness toward them. It is a sign of a possible return to my roots, relieved from the rubbish which has been inculcated in me, at the same time to a dimension I had buried for a long time, even though it was part of myself. I hesitate to call this dimension 'spirituality' because I am not too sure what is behind this word."

In some ways Alice's text speaks for itself. It is an interpretation of a life history as well as a life history itself. And I want to emphasize the fact that an educational biography is both. It expresses an adult's life but it is also always an interpretation of an adult's life written with the concern of education in mind. As a researcher, I will necessarily put this text in the framework of my own research, which is not exactly the same as Alice's research expectations. In working with students' individual biographies I tend to conduct two different tasks, to work at two different levels. I offer, through my understanding of biography, feedback or a contribution, like any other group member, to the understanding of each educational biography. We can share our views about each person's life and, in so doing, about the education of adults. My own research includes my frame of reference as well as all the research material I have been collecting over the years. The adults I work with are centered on their own biographies in light of what they learned from reading some research and what they shared in the small group. I work with each biography in the context of all the biographies I have heard and read and also with enlightenment from many other sources.

In the particular case of Alice, she knows she is coming back to something spiritual. She is witnessing herself moving in that direction. This return can be understood in the light of her own development and might be related to her age or to the present context of society. She says clearly that we come back in our lives to what has been part of our education but on our own terms. The enlargement of our cultural references does not mean that we abandon what has been meaningful in the past. We reconstruct what we already have. We adjust our needs to the demands of the context before us and can choose the context according to our demand. We are not educated until we can give meaning to our education—in some ways we are not educated until we can educate ourselves.

Summary

Adulthood can be seen as a process of finding one's autonomy in relation to family, schooling, and the sociocultural environment, the three contexts of emancipation often described in educational biographies.

Moving away or reacting against the family of one's childhood seems to be a necessary learning stage in the process of becoming an adult. Finding the right distance in relation to one's parents seems to be the result of a long, painful, and sometimes unending process.

Early schooling is not an important issue for adults as long as they did not have problems. Many adults, however, have had to mend a sense of failure they have been carrying in their relationship to knowledge. Schooling is primarily a social experience. The students remember relationships both with students and teachers more than specific curricula or examinations they have passed.

Adults educate themselves also in relation to the values of their earlier education. Most of the students I have researched, coming from rural areas more than cities and having had a religious education or other important social or personal experiences, have a system of values that has influenced their vocational choice and their understanding of society.

For adults learning is partly a process of finding their identity. Adults spend years working on understanding themselves, and the biographical process for those in such professions as teaching, nursing, or social work requires a deep self-knowledge. Traveling, living in another country, changing jobs, enrolling in continuing education, all are different ways of finding identity and coming to self-understanding.

Chapter Five

Exploring Adults' Ways of Thinking

One of the benefits of preparing an educational biography is that the process helps individuals clarify their frames of reference and interpret their approach to learning. Each adult's frame of reference is shaped by gender and by experiences in family, school, and community.

Each adult learner has his or her own relationship to knowledge, and this relationship is influenced by the social and cultural characteristics of the individual's life history. Traditionally, we have measured education in terms of products, and studies of adult learning have too often been centered on adapting formal teaching to meet adults' informational requirements. For most instructors, knowing still is centered on tests and diplomas. Adult knowledge is not considered valid until it can be controlled. Therefore research on adults' learning styles and ways of thinking is a recent focus in the study of adult learning. The way adults think often reveals their social background, the formal level of their education, and what they have experienced in their vocational as well as personal lives. This is why adults' ways of thinking have to be seen and analyzed in the context of their life history. There is a biographical foundation for the way adults think. When they analyze a situation, present their ideas about action, or share their reasons for behaving as they do, adults reveal their way of thinking about who they are and how they consider their lives.

Each adult seems to have a coherence in his or her way of thinking. Each individual follows a frame of reference, what Jack Mezirow (1991) terms a "meaning perspective" or "meaning scheme." This frame can be described as a kind of *structure* of interpretation, mediating the way the adult understands himself or herself and the world around him or her. The individual's educational biography expresses his or her global way of thinking. In short, it is probably necessary to deal with adult learning in the context of adults' frames of reference, which educational biographies reveal and help to explain.

Cognitive approaches to adult learning and much of the research addressing facilitation of adult learning are based on psychological or psychosociological studies, which differ from the biographical examination offered in this chapter. The cognitive approach, focused on reasoning about content or mastering a behavior, addresses the level of cognitive difficulty an adult is able to reach and the efficacy of his or her mental functioning. In his book *L'entretien d'explicitation* (The interview of explanation), French psychologist Pierre Vermersch (1994) developed a methodology to analyze errors made by adults in solving a problem or facing, for example, the breakdown of a machine. A specialist in the psychology of work, Vermersch is aware that "knowing the final result is not sufficient to diagnose the nature and the reason of a difficulty or an outstanding success" (p. 18). Thus, in order to understand what is implied in a behavior, Vermersch uses a technique of interviewing that helps a person remember and verbalize the stages of thinking he or she went through while taking an action: "the objective is to help the learner to explain in his or her own language, the content, the structure of his or her actions and his or her private way of thinking" (p. 25). This technique has been explored as a preventive approach in the world of technicians employed in nuclear powerhouses in France to detect the kind of thinking that lets them make mistakes. This technique is also helpful to researchers and educators in showing them how to maintain a self-discipline of listening in conducting an interview centered on the memory of past behavior. In this respect it does speak to the biographical approach.

The facilitating approach is mainly used by adult educators inspired by humanist psychology who want to relate their teaching or guidance to the goals of adult development. Facilitating can also be helpful in employing the biographical approach. Listening to an adult's life history with the aim of better grasping his or her way of thinking implies that researchers and educators should not project their own ideas into the adult's frame of reference, which is always more difficult than it seems, especially for instructors or adult educators. For example, because of the growing cultural gap between generations and the changing dynamic of family life, a young person's need to remain close to parents or family might be misunderstood. I know that I have a problem myself restraining myself from commenting on the basis of my own experience when I listen to young students who are anxious to keep a close relationship with their parents.

Although the cognitive and facilitative approaches are at times relevant to the ways adults think, my understanding of adults' ways of thinking is closer to Mezirow's meaning perspectives. I also agree with the categories he defines as "factors shaping a meaning perspective"— epistemic, sociolinguistic, and psychological—although I would not use the very same categories. Moreover, my biographical research leads me to emphasize the sociolinguistic dimension, which I consider very helpful for analyzing what we in the French world of adult education call the *adult relation to knowledge*. I make a distinction among what I consider the three sources of knowledge: science, tradition, and conviction, which are not too far from Mezirow's three notions mentioned above. Both these sets of sources of knowledge comprise a unified view of knowledge. The historical, social, and personal dimensions of thinking are taken together to form a whole. In the act of knowing, adults are presented with their social heritage and their level of education as well as the dynamics of their personal life itinerary. This is why I feel able to discuss the ambitious idea of a *structure* of interpretation, an *adult hermeneutics*.

I admit that for Mezirow and myself this view of the problem of understanding ways of adult thinking is largely influenced by the experience we have had for years in training adult educators, both within and outside the academic circle. We have both thought about adult learning in a variety of professional contexts, all centered on human relationships such as teaching, caring, or helping. We both have worked in the context of academic curricula in which the knowledge of oneself has had an important place. I am not saying that the position we are taking is biased by our workplace. I merely want to underline the population we mostly have in mind when we talk about identifying ways of thinking. I do not mean to say that auto mechanics with a few years of apprenticeship or highly qualified technicians will not have similar patterns. My findings might be true for them too, but I cannot ignore that I have built my concepts with students who have had a rather long and good education and who have made public service or training a priority.

Further, I am more preoccupied by the relevance of the ideas or hypotheses generated by the analysis of educational biographies than by any generalization based on quantitative data. In many ways it would not have been possible to start the research on educational biography without a population of adult students able to give meaning to their life course. Any kind of clinical knowledge is based upon critical cases. The subjects of the cases of psychoanalysis Freud chose to write about were not average adults. He wanted these cases to be conclusive of his position.

What Brookfield (1987) has written about learning within intimate relationships could be expanded to other areas of knowledge: "the formal study of learning is, as yet, relatively unexplored by educators." And he adds an observation that confirms what I have done for years with students by using the biographical approach: "assisting adults to become reflective learners within such relationships must be one of the most important functions which helping professionals can perform" (p. 74). Reflective learning is not only seldom explored, it is also extremely difficult to do. Most students are not used to exploring their way of thinking and have a hard time describing the way they have learned.

Josso (1991) examines this kind of learning in a book that discusses the study she has done with a group of students at the University of Geneva and her own work on her educational biography. She decided to work for a second year with a group of students who had prepared educational biographies, in order to identify the process of their ways of thinking. She also prepared a subtle interpretation of the dynamics of her own intellectual biography, as she calls it. The process of an adult's way of thinking, according to Josso, has two principles: the transformation of what happens in an adult life into a meaningful experience, and consciousness raising as an impetus and a result of the process. Preparing the biographical narrative is itself an experience that discloses a way of knowing. Comparing her own intellectual biography with all the biographies she has collected over the years, Josso identifies three different ways of knowing for adults: existential, pragmatic, and comprehensive. The existential way of learning is related to psychosomatic learning, the pragmatic with instrumental or relational learning, and the comprehensive with reflective learning. In each of these three types of learning, there are six categories of analysis: psychological, sociological, economic, psychosociological, political, and cultural, and Josso illustrates what she means by these different categories. For example, in the existential way of thinking, each category is associated with a type of personal interpretation. The psychological category might address a dream, stress, or suffering; the sociological category, professional identity; the economic category, life organization or budget; the psychosociological category, interpersonal relationships; the political category, decision making; and the cultural category, attitude toward nature. Josso's work is an extremely useful and accurate contribution, yet it is just the beginning of what we need in the formal study of learning.

The idea of a frame of reference is important in the field of education and the understanding of an adult frame of reference is central for adult education. The recognition that adults have their own ways of thinking is a starting point for any teaching objective. Packages of knowledge and educational CD-ROMs and multimedia products might be sold to adult learners, but their content will remain abstract as long as these learners do not make the effort to translate it into their own frames of reference. Working with adults implies an interpersonal and intercultural level of communication.

Adult educators should never assume they have an understanding of the population they speak to. They always have to remain open to the dynamics of communication; this openness is a basic rule for any work done with adults. Our understanding of adult learning belongs to the world of interpretation. As educators, we cannot control the way adults think. We can only approach adults' ways of thinking. We must make use of what I have called clinical knowledge in order to interpret or sometimes simply guess what we understand.

Because adult educators do not always have the time or the background for building their own frame of reference about adults' ways of thinking, in the following sections I review what I have learned from educational biographies. I do not mean to impose these ideas on any adult educator, but I share them as hypotheses I have found useful in my own interpretation of adults' ways of thinking.

Family Roots Contrasted to Popular and Scholarly Culture

Most of the adult students with whom I have worked are still adapting to an academic culture. Even when they are highly qualified or have some relevant knowledge, they often feel foreign in the academic environment. Consequently, many adults studying for a degree tend to mystify university life. They feel they do not quite belong to this academic culture. They have a difficult time with a language to which their family did not accustom them. This might be more true in Switzerland where there is less urbanization than in some other developed countries and where people maintain close ties with their family, social, and geographical environments. Indeed, some of my colleagues who have progressed through an academic career nevertheless act somewhat rebellious against the academic culture because of a perceived collusion between academic knowledge and the culture of the establishment. The cultural identity of scholars sometimes seems antisocial. They behave as though they do not want to belong to a sociocultural environment they do not really recognize. This seems more the case among professors of social science or science than among those in law or medicine.

Most adult learners' narratives begin with a brief description of the family environment. Students frequently mention their grandparents—the style of their lives and their work. They insist on mentioning family values or beliefs. In describing their education they associate their childhood with a local culture, often rural, in which their family plays a central role. They often show a tension, as one woman says, between an "inherited cultural identity and a conquered cultural identity." All students who were born in small towns or villages have strong roots in a popular culture associated with the culture of their family. Thinking about her education, one student, Helen, raised such questions as: "Where does my education start? From birth? From my parents' projects and desires? Or even before, in the family culture transmitted from generation to generation? In what sense is my education dependent upon a bigger history and a smaller history? How much is this education also dependent upon the phenomenon of repetition which, through side roads, strangely enough leads us finally to attitudes or choices similar to those of our parents?" She begins answering these questions in her educational biography: "I have been overawed by the importance of the roots and the layers on which my education has been established." And she offers the meaningful comment: "Should I say that I am pointing, in my narrative, to a determinism, or to the contrary do I recognize some specific dimensions of my own identity?"

Culture affects the process of education. Most life histories reflect intercultural dimensions. A few years ago, I found in the biographies a contrast between a rural culture deeply rooted in ancestral traditions and the modern style of life found in urban areas. Today the intercultural dynamic is related more to migration, floods of refugees, and the internationalization of the work market. Many adults have to adapt to another culture, to a culture they were not prepared to face, and this process of change becomes partly a process of education. Indeed, they have to learn a language other than their mother tongue. They have to understand new rules and learn new behaviors. They have to adapt to new values and another type of social organization.

Helen writes: "My childhood has its roots in a world almost medieval, and it is not by chance that my research projects when I was studying history were centered on the Middle Ages. This childhood seems to me very distant and looks like a former life. It is true that nothing is similar in my actual environment, especially with basic dimensions like my relation with space and time, whether it means time or weather." At the same time she has inherited a hotel in the Alps, where she had spent most of her summers during her childhood and youth. This hotel used to be totally isolated but because of an electric power project became accessible to buses and cars. When her parents died Helen made the decision to take over the hotel and keep it open from June to October, in addition to her jobs as a secondary school teacher and as the mother of three children. Of her attachment to this place, she writes: "This hotel is a primitive place as well as a place of modern techniques. A place for rules and their transgression (I have been told stories of smugglers and poachers). It is the place of my father and mother. It is also a frontier, the end of the road and near to the Italian border. This place represents for me a kind of umbilical cord that I have not been able, so far, to cut."

Such attachment to a land, an environment, a culture influences an adult's way of thinking. It regulates life with the dynamics of both tradition and change. Adults' lives are rooted in the past, but in order to build their own lives they have to open a path to a new horizon and work on their own understanding of the world. What Helen writes is very meaningful: "Moving from a culture of permanence or essence to a culture of progress or change, I have been completely a woman of my time although I have kept inside myself something from another time. What I learned as a child remains and forms the layers against which I still learn today." Culture is also for many adults tied to the geographical environment. The harmony of the rural context of childhood might even influence a person's occupational choice. In one narrative, a woman expressed the contrast she felt between what she learned from nature and what she had to discover in an urban environment.

> I remember what I have learned: odor, color, warmth. All I have learned, I have learned by myself, by observing, by a life close to nature. I was drawn to the simplicity of life, taking part naturally in life, death, and suffering. . . . I have a nostalgia for a knowledge I can pull directly out of life and not from a theory or a discourse. I wish I could still learn from nature and not be obliged to go back to school because it sounds up to date. I wish I could still learn by being crea-tive, by doing by myself, by observing somebody do something in-stead of asking for an explanation.

Sometimes the regulation is provoked by a rupture such as leav-ing home or experiencing any rapid change of social environment, a time abroad in the Third World, perhaps, or a period in a tempo-rary job. Let's take an example from Claire's narrative:

> My stay in Quito was quite something. I had to face all kinds of new realities and ways of life, at different levels: personal, familial, emo-tional, social, political, cultural, and economic. I had to put my clocks back in time. The family with whom I stayed in Quito gave me the opportunity to look back and value differently my own fam-ily, especially as far as the relationship between mother and daugh-ter was concerned. Some typical values in Equador gave me new ideas about the values of my own country. I had a new frame of ref-erence, a general view which helped me look at my life and my aspi-rations in a new way.

Coming from a family which found refuge in Switzerland, Maria offers in her life history another example of a cultural background that is part of family tradition. Having mixed cultural roots, and be-ing part Jewish and part colored, Maria writes: "The family story I have experienced and been told about has taught me the different possible ways to lead a life and to explain life's events. . . . In my life I am looking for diversity, and I cannot accept dogmatism in the way we understand reality. I am seduced by differences, and I reject any kind of imposed norm." She also understands that both her attraction to art and esthetics and her choice of nursing as a career are the result of the culture and values inherited from her family: "I always felt a need for an artistic life." Further, she adds that "the suffering of the uprooted members of my family, who also had to face economic difficulties, has led me to be sensitive to others."

In the educational biographies I have analyzed, most adults seem to have found their identity by reacting against their cultural heritage. They have tried other ways of thinking, counter-models through which they have experienced other languages such as those of religious belief or political commitment. They have built their values and references by exploring differences, going beyond the norms of their education, traveling in Third World countries, living and working abroad, or moving from a rural area to the city. Social experiences have been the key to explaining the different stages of their ways of thinking. As one student writes: "I believe all my traveling, in my country and abroad, has been in search of my cultural identity, a sort of checking of my roots."

In my research I have mostly worked with adults between thirty and forty years of age who grew up in Europe after the end of the Second World War and during the national liberation movements of Third World countries. Their adulthood has been dominated by the idea that education is central to life and opens access to the job market. These adults built their professional careers before the economic difficulties of the last decade. Their social experiences belong, therefore, to their generation. Younger adults will certainly be responding to a different cultural heritage. Today, because of the economic instability and the high level of unemployment, their reaction might be more conformist and less influenced by social movements, but like everyone else, they will need cultural references in order to choose what they want from their lives. What matters for me here of course is not a comparative study of these two generations, but the idea that we all construct our way of thinking through a reorganization of our cultural heritage.

School and the Process of Thinking

Mostly biographies follow a chronological pattern. My content analysis shows interactions between the different scenes in a common process of growing and learning. There is, for example, an obvious interaction between family and school. This sociocultural cohesiveness between family and school has a crucial impact on schooling. The children of educated parents identify themselves as students from the beginning of their school years and have problems with social identity when they fail in their classes. The other children are more dependent on their parents' willingness to encourage them to study or on their parents' other expectations for their schooling and future lives. After being obliged to drop out of school for some years, Matthias writes: "By going back to school, I will meet my family's expectations, and I will again be my parents' 'preferred child.'" A counter-example comes from Elizabeth's narrative: "School is a place of suffering which reveals my weakness: I do not like to read, I am very bad with orthography. . . . I swallow the image given to me by my family and teacher. At this time of my life, I am convinced that I am not clever and that I am one of the worst students in the class. That is the way it is." For many parents the success of their children at school gives them an indication of what to expect for the children's future. The parents' feedback then plays an important role in the way children see themselves as students.

I have understood from the adult biographies that success or failure in school takes on a deep symbolism. In other words, the interpretation of the result is as important as the result itself. The self-image individuals acquire as a result of their schooling therefore has a continuing strong effect on the way they see themselves as adults. Family and school are sources of reinforcement for crucial choices made throughout the life course. The culture of their family has an influence on the way adults manage the level of success or failure they obtained during the school years. Their interpretation of their school education is a key reference for their level of self-esteem. Their choice of a professional life is often a consequence of this interpretation. Continuing education, therefore, may be taken to mean more than taking formal coursework as an adult. It can also express the idea that the effects of education in younger years indeed continue through adulthood. And it remains extremely difficult to modify the way adults think about themselves as learners.

Furthermore, the evaluation processes students encounter during their school years have a tendency to freeze their interpretation of their ability to think. Grades are taken as a sentence. What one woman says of the feeling of failure she experienced in high school tells us how strong such feelings can remain: "By studying at the university, I thought that I could heal an old wound. It has not been the case. There is a fault in my schooling which troubles my relation with myself. I will never forget this failure: it bothers my decision-making process and limits my boldness." (I come back to the theme of evaluation in Chapter Eight.)

Good students may understand the meaning of their success within the larger culture of their education. This culture is often the culture of a group or a social class. Once individuals identify with a culture, they are consequently limited by the constraints of that culture. For many adults the dynamics of their socialization are associated with cultural differences. In the narratives I analyzed, for instance, several adults describe the shock they felt when discovering that the culture at a school was associated with a social class. "I do not find my place among sons and daughters of ministers, doctors, lawyers, and teachers," says a woman when she describes the first year she spent as a student in a school of medicine before choosing to study sociology. This kind of statement is repeated quite often and is made of high schools as well as schools of higher education.

Thus an adult's way of thinking is usually the result of choices made earlier in life in reaction to events and situations. Failure as well as success, punishment as well as praise, fear as well as favor have been the sources of the norms through which learning has taken place, and they have become templates for the adult's way of thinking. Schooling points out a paradigm. There is always a social environment to set limits and dictate the norms of correct behavior. Adults construct their way of thinking through the dynamics of their socialization. They follow other people's thinking or they react strongly against it or deviate from the collective ways of thinking. In the narratives, some people explain how they have been rejected because of their ideas and how they have moved out of the collective ways of thinking of the church, political, sport, and other groups to which they once belonged.

Adult education can question the meaning given to schooling. It can be defined as an opportunity to conform to the requirements of formal education as well as to transform a way of thinking. Although the cumulative knowledge learned at school is often a part of the basis on which adults have built their way of thinking, new learnings do not necessarily mean that an adult's way of thinking will change. Adult education might challenge an existing background or it might not. It might lead adults to other approaches to knowledge or make them resist new approaches. The continuing influence of school may either qualify or disqualify. Insufficiency of schooling might be a motivation for continuing one's education or a reason to reject further education. The educational biography is an opportunity for adult learners to interpret the period they spent at school, to give or take away support for the meanings they have given to their school background and their existing ways of thinking.

Finally, for the adult women in my classes at the University of Geneva, schooling is associated with a culture and a socialization predominantly directed by and for men and therefore not completely theirs. In their narratives most of them associate a kind of strangeness with the academic way of thinking. I return to this issue later in this chapter.

Occupation as a Source of Intellectual Obedience

After some years of reading educational biographies, I tried, in the midst of my content analysis, to compare all the narratives I had. In this comparison I noticed a clear difference between the nurses and the rest of the women. The nurses' involvement in their occupation began early in life, as soon as they started nursing school. In their narratives, they defined their work either as a commitment that they had had difficulty leaving or, to the contrary, as a very demanding job, one that they were happy to leave for a while. They identified as nurses with an occupation, a social group, and a culture. The history of their profession and its status within the medical profession have an influence on the image they have of themselves. It might sound condescending to say that nurses have a way of thinking, but it is not far from the truth. This has been confirmed to me many times. Nurses comply with a collective way of thinking that has evolved over the years but remains grounded in basic principles and common theories. Regardless of what they are asked to do by their superiors, many nurses act according to their own tacit knowledge. Thus, in more general terms, a person's way of thinking is associated with his or her occupational training and practice in the workplace. If there is a cultural attachment to family roots, there are also cultural bonds growing out of years spent in an occupation.

In the world of adult educators these cultural differences become obvious to me each time I have to teach or work in a training group. Nurses are not the only class or group of adults who have a common way of thinking. Social workers, for example, raise the same types of questions about their instructions. Schoolteachers share similar reactions, and their teaching may differ from school regulations. Managers have similar attitudes toward their organizations. These sociocultural conditions affecting adult ways of thinking exist for many other professions.

Adults also think according to the epistemological assumptions prevailing in their profession. This is true for nurses, doctors, lawyers, engineers, and technicians, among others. In his biographical narrative, for example, a professor of medicine working mainly in the field of patient education explains very clearly how he had had to shift his scientific view in order to be able to deal with patient learning. He had to change the physio-pathological approach to patients that had been his professional way of thinking. Another adult educator who had worked for many years as an engineer described how he had to develop new knowledge and attitudes in order to understand phenomena that were completely out of his field, such as group dynamics and adult development.

Adult educators, according to the research done by Josso and her colleagues, including myself (Josso, Bausch, Dominicé, and Finger, 1990), come from a variety of sociocultural and school backgrounds, often with a university doctoral degree and sometimes having served an apprenticeship in training. As they enter the field of adult education as professionals, they tend to adopt similar ways of thinking. In our research we have found that adult educators agree they have types of abilities in common, such as intellectual curiosity, professional competence, and an interest in self-development. They recognize a drive for independence and autonomy in themselves. As one of them says: "I am always keeping a door open in case I need to quit my job and look for another employer." This common way of thinking about their job illustrates how the context of working life can influence adults' ways of thinking.

In the article she wrote at the end of our research, Josso identified three categories of knowledge, which she discusses more fully in her book (1991), into which the group of adult educators sorted the key qualifications for their job: pragmatic and instrumental knowledge, existential knowledge, and comprehensive or explicative knowledge. They also identified personal experience, educational experience, and professional experience as the three sources of learning that establish their basic skills as adult educators. This profession is especially interesting to me because it is a new profession for which a clear profile is difficult to draw. It is a profession for which we can still find pioneers, like the ones we had for our research. Adult educators have been able up until now to create their jobs or to assist in constructing the profile of their profession. For older professions the norms are so well established that there is little margin for a professional to develop his or her own way of thinking. Professional codes and organizational requirements have the most control over the way employees think about their job. If they do not conform to the norms they are asked to follow and to which the organization is committed, their position will be questioned, and they may lose their jobs. It would be interesting to analyze situations in which managers, employees, and workers have to identify with an organization, follow its norms, and adapt to its values. It would surely illustrate how adults tend to think according to the rules to which they are supposed to conform and how they have internalized a way of thinking through their working lives.

I do not know of any research dealing with the mutual influence of professional and personal experiences. Are we looking at ourselves or the world from a professional point of view? In what direction does the transfer work: from personal to professional or the other way around? The boundaries we have made in our societies between professional and personal and between public attitudes and private ones obscure the systemic approach to which I refer. It is again the question of what comes first, the chicken or the egg? Research in the field of guidance and counseling explains how an occupational choice combines psychological and sociological aspects. But the interactions between this choice and other choices in life lead to another type of problem. In the epistemic, sociolinguistic, and psychological factors identified by Mezirow (1991) that shape meaning perspectives, the challenge is precisely to understand the interaction between these factors. In what order are they organized, and what are the dynamics of interaction between these three factors in the course of one's life?

A good answer to these questions will require an interdisciplinary approach to research. The educational biography could contribute to it, but the narrative would have to be centered on this specific object of research. For the cluster of adult educators my colleagues and I were researching, it is possible to stress a mutual influence between the profession they have chosen and the person each of them is. On the one hand, for some of them, being a professional adult educator has been a clear choice made in order to be more authentic or to fit with personal values or a point of view about society. This choice can be interpreted as a way to adapt their professional involvement to the person they have become. On the other hand they recognize how much this commitment has influenced their personal life. As Eric told us in his narrative: "I am trying as much as possible to work according to my ideas and my person. . . . My experience as an engineer in a company made me aware that in the long run, the person and the work should fit. Being an adult educator has been a way to be closer to my inner deeper self and my personal path."

Men's and Women's Ways of Thinking

Should we identify women's ways of thinking and women's ways of writing in the presentation of educational biography? These types of questions are still open, and the studies about them are quite recent. Without going into detail about the differences between men and women as expressed in their narratives, I have observed some general trends. Men enter their working lives at the primary school level. They take grades as a guide to the professional choice they must eventually make. A woman's situation is more complex, encompassing, as one woman said, "woman, spouse, mother, and professional." If the men are able to keep the different aspects of their lives separate, the women are mostly thinking of themselves as unified persons. If most men like tactics and do not fear competition, women are more able to break through barriers in order to obtain what they want. When women study later in their lives, they need to share their doubts about themselves as students and about their ability to think by themselves.

As Mary says in her narrative when she describes coming back to the university: "My decision to study again has been an answer to a vital need, a kind of reflex of survival, interior survival for the search of an identity and my own way of thinking and acting. I cannot grow without building autonomy in my way of thinking and the ability to express it. It is a kind of fight to discover a place which is mine and not the one other people wish me to take." The inherited models of the past are often mentioned by women, who define their search for identity through the image of the will and the fight to defend their own ideas.

The women whose educational biographies I have heard and read are clearly the witnesses to a social and cultural change. With the women's liberation movement, that broad social movement which influenced the models of education and the process of socialization prevailing in most of our societies, a new culture for women has emerged (Oliveira, 1989). This culture has also had an effect on the model guiding men's social and cultural development. There is a great deal of literature today on male and female cultures, and I recognize a difference between genders in the way adults think. We know from the work of Jung that the boundary between male and female is not absolute, but for sociological reasons it seems to me necessary to underline this difference and to proclaim to adult educators that it is not always taken into consideration.

Some years ago I asked a group of women to work specifically as women on the interpretation of their narratives. They made some interesting comments. These women developed another idea of adulthood. They were afraid to detach themselves from a child-like side, which society has traditionally considered part of their identity. They felt they had to grow socially in a world of men in which they found it difficult to keep their own ways of thinking. The academic world is dominated by men's ways of thinking. This might cause the difficulty the women reported of losing themselves by succeeding in their studies. Education is closely connected with power. This group of women found a closeness between the powerlessness of children and their own lack of power. As they wrote:

"We have all, though differently, tried to gain power in our lives, through conflict, flirtation, seduction, choosing situations of independence and leadership, gaining a better knowledge about the role women play in society and power." They also noticed in their report how much "a woman has to identify with male desire, with how women are valued by men or by women in a man's role." They see women's studying at an older age as being partly influenced by this compulsion. They also emphasized that they had an ambiguous image of their mothers that did not help them to have a clear autonomy or to be proud of their way of thinking.

In further work I will try to deepen this research because I believe it is a key dimension of adult ways of thinking that has been completely neglected over the centuries. The literature on this matter is just beginning to appear (Tennant and Pogson, 1995). Tennant and Pogson call Carol Gilligan (1982) "a pioneer critic of the gender bias." Her book is one of the few contributions that presents "another way" of adult thinking. The issue of gender remains an important challenge for the future of continuing education.

In this chapter I have not addressed the problem of transforming adult ways of thinking. I admire the attention given by Mezirow in his brilliant book (1991) to the subtle process of perspective transformation. In spite of his clear and challenging reasoning, I sometimes found the detailed explanation of this process a little too abstract. The wonderful effort made by Patricia Cranton (1995) in her book devoted to Mezirow's ideas, tends on the contrary to be too pragmatic. Consequently, in an attempt to avoid falling into either of these traps, my purpose has been more to convince adult educators to be open to the diversity of adults' ways of thinking than to tell them how to use this diversity in their teaching or educational action. The learning process, I believe, is the responsibility of the adult himself or herself. What I call in French the *formative* process is characterized by each adult's educational biography. This is the lesson I have learned from my students' biographical testimonies. Our task as adult educators is to help each adult develop his or her own creative way of thinking. How can we accomplish this goal if we do not endeavor to empower adults' ways of thinking by all means and even by challenging them? By enriching men's and women's ways of thinking, adult education might open new ways of looking at the future of our societies. This principle has to be received as a paradox in a world of continuing education more and more dominated by the selling of packaged one-size-fits-all educational programs.

Summary

Educational biographies reveal that each adult has a frame of reference, a way of thinking, a cohesiveness that can be understood as a type of structure of interpretation. These adult ways of thinking include more than the cognitive dimension necessary for mastering a specific content or solving a problem. They also have cultural roots.

Families tend to shape the cultural roots of adult ways of thinking. Parents have projects for their children. They interfere with their schooling whatever the grades they obtain. They influence their vocational choices and even the personal decisions they make about their emotional lives. Adults spend their lives trying to build, on the basis of this foundation, their own ways of thinking.

Schools determine the self-image of learners. Schooling is a process of carving a path through parents' desires and school success or failure. Learning takes place as a process of socialization and resembles a process of acquiring social identity. Whether learners choose the world of technical expertise, literature, or business, they come to partake of an occupational way of thinking. Also, the context in which they work imposes the references of an organizational culture. Nurses, for example, have the way of thinking of their profession. Adult educators and those in many other professions also tend to follow the thinking patterns of their chosen profession.

Recent research takes gender characteristics seriously. Men and women have differences in their ways of thinking. Along with these different gender characteristics exist different cultural characteristics, and all this diversity in people's traits should be taken seriously by the various techniques of adult education. This is a lesson learned from the plural relationships to knowledge appearing in the educational biographies.

Chapter Six

Learners' Needs, Motivations, and Dreams

Personal interviews conducted during research on the motivation for continuing education among employees who wanted to acquire a diploma after having worked for several years in banks or insurance companies clearly show a complex and sometimes contradictory expression of needs among adult learners: "[I needed] to prove to people that I was able to do something else. In fact I need people around me to say, 'this woman is after all a good woman.'" "I wanted to continue studying after being forced to quit after my daughter's birth." "In today's society it is necessary to be enrolled in a program of continuing education. I decided to pursue this diploma for secretarial work in business administration because it is well recognized in the world of work." "I need to get busy. I have nobody in my life. Therefore I need to fill a emptiness. Instead of going out every night, I would rather do something useful."

What is the adult learner's motivation for enrolling in an educational program? How can adult learning needs be identified through a study of adults' life experiences? What is the place of continuing education in the attainment of a long-term personal goal? The majority of instructors working with adults consider an understanding of adult educational needs an essential part of teaching, but they do not always know how to ascertain their students' real motivations. The adults themselves are very often unclear about their motivations when they register for an educational program. Sometimes they realize only months or even years later what they were really looking for. Discovering the adult learner's motivation for learning is important for both the instructor and the learner.

Adults have all kinds of reasons for going back to school, and the motivation to pass an exam or to obtain a degree does not cover the whole sphere of their learning needs. Even when adult educators use andragogical techniques to help their students express their needs and motivations for learning, they often focus only on needs that relate to the content of the teaching offered. Therefore, in conjunction with other tools, the educational biography is a useful approach to determining needs because it seeks those needs and motivations in the global context of the adult's life history.

The Organization of Needs in Adult Education

In recent decades adult education has served all kinds of adults—migrant workers, specialized workers, women reentering the workforce, top managers, and the elderly. Although it remains a kind of public service, it must also be considered more and more a public market. Consequently, the strategies of most adult education currently have more to do with meeting the expressed needs of adults rather than with helping them to uncover their real motivations.

Today the responsibility of the adult educator includes gaining a clear idea of adults' motivations in order to understand their reasons for choosing a certain educational product or to better grasp the meaning of their decision to learn some specific subject or skill. In most programs in adult education, it is assumed that the learners' needs have been recognized. Adult educators who are professionals in charge of successful programs are assumed to have fully analyzed the motivations of the adults enrolled in their classes in order to offer them what they really want to learn. However, we need to look more closely at what we are actually learning about learners, at the forces that can affect the expression of their needs and motivations, and at the role educational biographies might play in revealing those needs and motivations more accurately.

The evolution of adult and continuing education in recent years has included the development of procedures to assess adults' educational needs. Members of the medical profession are aware that certain adult patients need information about managing particular diseases, and they might ask the patient to attend a seminar on the subject of diabetes, for example. Psychologists offer a panoply of workshops on human relations because they recognize the needs of people in many professions to become more conscious of the dynamics of interpersonal communication and relations. "For your own good," as Alice Miller (1983; my translation) said, is the sentence often used by a human resource development manager when he tells his employees to select an educational activity from a catalogue.

Adult education seeks to respond to our educational needs at various stages in our lives: when we need to change jobs, when we raise our children, when our bodies require the discipline of exercise, when we retire, and when in old age we try to preserve our independence. For whatever we need to learn about housing, electronics, or music or whenever we are facing a problem such as finding a school for a child, planning a vacation, or borrowing money, we can attend a group, meet a counselor, or read pertinent guides or manuals. Ways to meet these kinds of needs are so well organized that there is always an answer, sometimes even before we can raise the question.

Of course the adult and continuing education market carries with it the same ambiguity as any other market: the client has the freedom to choose the product best suited to his or her own needs, which means that he or she will analyze those needs through the filter of the kinds of adult education opportunities offered and the ways they are presented in brochures or catalogues. Adults tend to ask how they can benefit from the market of adult education before questioning or even instead of questioning the dimensions of their need. The consumer society structures our needs by pointing out ways in which we can take advantage of what is currently being sold on the market. The education of adults as clients of educational programs prevails over the analysis of their personal needs. When a subject is not offered in an adult education program, when the need for it is not recognized by the system of adult education, individuals may not recognize this need in themselves either. The poorly educated take courses that others consider they need, the more ambitious take those that are supposed to help them advance, and the well educated let the university tell them what new scientific discoveries or cultural research they should study.

Adults today often have a series of courses, workshops, and seminars that they have to follow or that they have completed. In European countries such as France, the budget devoted to such continuing education by recent legislation gives many employees and workers the opportunity to further their learning. The extensiveness of the resulting educational market for adults has made guidance and counseling and of course needs assessment a standard preliminary phase of adult education. In this growing market and its assessment procedures, educational biographies could be an interesting source of information because they describe the ways in which adults actually make use of various types of adult and continuing education. Short versions of biographical narratives could be prepared and analyzed in the process of needs assessment as a way to enlarge the horizon of needs in adult education to match the context of a life history. The structure of workshops offered by Ginette Robin (1992) is a good example of such a procedure.

Educational program needs should not be opposed to internal, or personal, needs, but in the dynamics of learning it should be clear that adults' expectations are often produced by the organization of adult and continuing education. Instead of having high expectations for adults' autonomy, the teacher or instructor of a class or workshop should recognize that most adults do not reflect that there may be a difference between what they are asked to do and what they want to accomplish. They look at themselves through the eyes of others; they understand the main events of their lives in light of how they have been perceived as adults. The need to be educated interacts with the need to affirm one's own way of thinking, of acting, and of being. There is a dialectic between what Pineau (1983) calls "auto-hetero formation," between the Piagetian idea of heteronomy and the concept of autonomy in psychosocial development, a dialectic expanded upon by Lawrence Kohlberg and some of his colleagues.

Adult needs are also influenced by the roles adults play in society: professional roles, family roles, and other social roles. Before people retire, they need to prepare themselves for a new stage of life; as parents, they need to understand the reactions of their children in order to foster child development; as citizens, they need to gather information in order to know what they are voting for. The public side of these roles modifies the expression of individual needs. In the context of work, for example, an individual's personal needs are often not given much weight if meeting them appears to benefit mainly that individual and not others as well. Similarly, some members of a community might oppose the needs expressed by other citizens for a day nursery or a swimming pool if they think that the project is in the interests of only a minority. Needs are subject to the cultural norms of social roles, and some may remain unexpressed in one social context yet be recognized and approved in another.

Finally, adults involved in an educational activity may be embarrassed by questions designed to uncover their personal motivations if they are accustomed to a more indirect approach to assessing their needs. Social order is not only interpreted by the law and enforced by the police, it is also maintained more subtly by social expectations and contexts, including educational activities. I experienced this phenomenon myself as a teacher when I was asked by a group of social workers to facilitate their work in a continuing education program that they had decided to turn into an experiment in self-managed learning. They did not like the teacher in charge of the program and had not found the course relevant. They unanimously decided to define by themselves what they really needed to learn and to drop the curriculum planned for them. It was a fascinating but traumatic experience for me, mainly because they did not know how to build a program that would meet their own needs or how to manage individual needs in a group setting. To explain this lack of knowledge and the reasons why they could not easily define an educational activity according to their own needs, several of the students made reference to the educational dependency of their school years and previous training.

Adults are so used to having someone else think and plan for them in educational settings that they are lost when they have to make these decisions for themselves rather than simply adjusting to a program. During my educational biography seminars, I am always struck by adult students' lack of reflection on their various educational experiences. They can make a list of the courses they have taken during their school and university years; they can describe what they have learned about society and themselves during the critical times in their lives. They have, however, a real difficulty in finding the thread that holds the pieces together. They can state the needs underlying the choices they have made at particular stages of their lives, but they have a difficult time interpreting these needs in terms of the dynamics of their life histories. In the field of adult education, therefore, adults' needs should typically be understood as reactions or responses made within the framework of the type of education being offered rather than as the expression solely of the learners' own wishes or personal goals. Because of the attitudes of dependency they have developed during their school years, adults are ordinarily neither inclined nor able to express a purely personal point of view regarding their educational needs.

The Motivation to Learn

Increasingly, instead of putting a lot of effort into trying to discover participants' personal needs and motivations for enrolling in a particular course of study, adult educators are seeking instructional approaches that will encourage adults to become active learners. That is, they take the participants' need to learn for granted and focus mainly on participant behavior in the class or workshop. Instructors want to know how to encourage learners to be more responsive, how to create a climate for cooperation, how to help learners confront their doubts and, as they become more secure, how to help them succeed in whatever the class requires. Learner motivation has become more of a challenge for the teachers than for the students. Even when adult educators see themselves primarily as facilitators, they must think about the dynamics of the situation, planning how to help adults move ahead, how to encourage them to change.

Much of the literature on adult learning argues that we cannot motivate other people but only inspire them to become motivated, to enhance their motivation to learn. This position reflects a mostly psychological understanding of learning. Throughout the history of education, teachers and others have advocated that learners must be active and in charge of their learning process. However, this cannot happen when learning is only a means to succeed in a program of continuing education. Instead, we need a new way to organize learning activities.

Currently, the motivation of the adult educator has become, as is already the case for the teacher in the school environment, the main factor in the adult student's motivation. Indeed, the ideas, the principles, and the intentions of an adult educator can increase or interfere with learner motivation. An enthusiastic teacher can greatly motivate an adult to learn. It is in fact impossible for the motivation of a participant not to be influenced by the motivation of an adult educator. Therein lies the potential interest as well as the burden of any educational situation for the instructor. The instructional relationship is a key factor in learner motivation.

As the number of adult education programs has greatly increased during the last decade and as these programs, with the generalization of continuing education, have become more centered on vocational qualifications, the identification of adult motivation in learning has become more of a pedagogical problem enclosed in the dynamics of teaching adults than a psychosociological open question to be analyzed in light of adult socialization or adult development. This is not to minimize the role played by the techniques used by an instructor to enhance student commitment but rather to underline the tendency in the institutionalization of adult education to reduce the learning process to the act of mastering the educational objectives of a program or of successfully recalling the content of a course. Today, adult education is often reduced to adult schooling.

Educational biographies reveal adults' profound lack of motivation for formal learning during the school years. The motivation for staying in school comes primarily from parents, sometimes from teachers, and occasionally from a student's vague idea about what he or she wants to become in the future. What motivation there is to learn never escapes the context of interpersonal relationships. One student wrote of one of his teachers: "I learned to please someone who in return favored me." Another described how the motivation to be a good student was a reaction against the parents' anti-school attitude: "As I discovered new things, alternative models, alternative futures, my first opposition to my parents' plans for me was to get good grades." This motivation arises not from the subjects themselves but as a reaction to the expectation of others. Good students may express doubts about their motivations when they look at their school histories. As one of them stated: "I have inside me the fuzzy but real impression that I was not the author of my own education during my studies; I feel I let myself be molded according to the wishes of my teachers without making the knowledge I acquired my own." These adults wondered if they were listening to their own needs while they were attending school.

In most cases the authors of such biographies expressed the inner conflict they were gradually discovering between successfully adapting to the requirements of organized educational needs that were assumed to be their own and fulfilling their more personal and hidden needs, sometimes frightening to themselves as well as to their associates. This conflict, which is very difficult to resolve, characterizes the education of students who now that they are no longer children or teenagers are typically free to abandon a program at any time. Adults enjoy being inspired by others, including their instructors, but at a deeper level, they want to discover and understand their own needs; they want to learn who they are. Educators and instructors should be aware of these two different levels of motivation among their adult students, especially at the time these students reenter the world of formal education.

The Need to Dream

Promoters of adult education influence adult learning needs with publicity that points out what adults should know and plays upon the wish to start a new life, to be elsewhere, or to explore one's hidden side. However, even if travel agencies and part-time employment offices promise the fulfillment of one's dreams, it should be obvious to anyone that the main characteristic of dreams is the impossibility of their fulfillment. Adult educators should realize that in any kind of educational situation, many participants have expectations that are deeply rooted in unconscious longings. Hidden behind wishes, there are inexpressible desires: dreams belong to the realm of needs, to that deeper level of motivation that adults cannot express.

As a university teacher, I have experienced the considerable extent to which adults who have not attended university earlier in life are impressed, sometimes scared, and sometimes proud once accepted as students. Some of them have the idea that they are fulfilling a great dream. When some months later they begin to feel more at home at the university, they speak about the demystification of their first impression. Dream becomes reality, but reality is not exactly like the dream. In addition to being the source of the motivation to study and to follow the set curriculum, the dream contains a more sacred view of knowledge, nourished by a vision of unattainable wisdom. Students' comments about their university program contain evidence that their positive statements include this symbolic dimension. In other words the dream is present when the students evaluate, in light of what they achieved in the program, the satisfaction of their needs.

In trying to discover a student's learning needs, adult educators should be aware of this gap between the reasons given for attending a class and the desire to go beyond the limits of the class. An organized educational activity can only partially meet the needs of the students, and thus students' pleasure in being motivated is related to the ability of a teacher or an instructor to help them reach out beyond the limits of a program. In addition, the trouble or anxiety and especially the fear of failure felt by adult students at the time of an examination can arise from the adult's own high expectations, shaped not only by personal needs but by an environment of severe judgments. The complexity of identifying these varied levels of adult learning needs reveals the oddity of the idea that scientific studies will enable adult educators to fully comprehend adults' educational expectations.

In a seminar focused on evaluation in adult education, I asked a small group of students reaching the end of their studies to participate in an experiment concerning the learning process and based on their own experiences. As a first step in this experiment, a group of five students tried to recall their motivation when they began the program. They came up with a list that they tested on other students attending the same seminar. This inquiry had little scientific value because it was not expanded to other groups, but it showed very clearly that educational needs in this group included very different and sometimes contradictory aspects. The need to enlarge one's theoretical references in order to improve professional practice went hand in hand with the need to discover new ways of thinking, the need to qualify for another job, and the need to be taken seriously by one's employer. Some students also mentioned another set of needs common to students in many programs, needs concerning the amount of time required for studying, the personal qualities desired in the teacher, and the opportunities for socialization offered by the class. In other words the need to study or to obtain a degree involves functional or concrete needs, such as requirements that can be met with the time or energy available and opportunities for personal development or the enrichment of social life. The diversity of needs that must be taken into account in an educational activity reflects the diversity of roles played by each adult. These needs may also be an expression of the contradictions of daily life, in which, for example, personal needs are often in conflict with professional needs.

We must all discover in the process of growing older what to do about contradictory needs, how to avoid frustration and achieve satisfaction, how to combine, for example, theoretical and experiential learning or formal schooling and more creative forms of learning. Students' narratives again give us good illustrations. They tell us that academic knowledge is taken seriously and even serves as a norm in the evaluation of teaching but that learning comes primarily from meaningful experiences. The demand for concrete lectures as a learning approach does not exclude group discussion, which may be the only way in which to give substance and practical meaning to a theory. The worth of traditional evaluation as a confirmation of real learning is often rejected. The knowledge gained by adults must, however, be acknowledged by society even though adults might claim to be responsible for their own learning. Adult educators and instructors should know that adulthood is full of contradictions and that these contradictions matter in the context of educational activities. Again, educational biographies are testimonies of these contradictions, as they are of the complexities of students' motivations, needs, and dreams.

Stages in the Evolution of Motivation

What typical needs assessment can do is to give us a good picture of what is expected by a given group of adults in a particular context and at a specific time. It can give relevance to the organization of educational activities. However, if we move from the organization of education to the behavior of the adult learner, as presented in his or her life history, we observe that the adult's need to learn evolves progressively over the years. The motivation of adults in continuing their education must be considered in light of these biographical dynamics and not only in term of what is offered. Many adults drop out of the programs they have chosen when they realize that the course content is not meeting their needs at this particular stage in their lives. Sometimes they are trying to use adult education as an escape from other problems in their lives, or they have underestimated the difficulties of returning to education. The adult educator or instructor must consider adult motivation for learning as a growing or maturing motivation. There is a right time in life for the right motivation. This view of motivation does not imply a linear process, however, but a dynamic pattern with special moments and stages before any decision or change is made. The idea of transition as presented by Levinson (1978) may be helpful in understanding this maturation, as may be the idea of life phases and stages as discussed in Chapter Three. Adults are sometimes not aware of the timing of their motivations; they often discover it by trial and error. Their initial enrollment in an adult education program may very well be their way of testing the current level of their motivation to learn.

Instructors should be aware of the extent to which they can and cannot motivate adults who are not ready to learn what is offered in an educational activity. Many examples could be mentioned because this question arises among adult educators in any discussion group; however, the example of patient education is particularly relevant. Patients attending a seminar in order to learn more about a chronic disease may feel out of place because they are still at the stage of denying their disease. They do not want to learn about a disease that they have not yet admitted to having. In the diabetes treatment and therapeutic teaching division at Geneva University General Hospital, Professor Jean Philippe Assal, with whom I have been associated as a consultant for many years, was forced to conclude that even when learning is vital for a patient, teaching is a waste of time if the motivation to learn has not matured.

At the university I have observed cycles of motivation. An evaluation of the learning process at the university level, made by the students themselves several years ago, made me realize that students' motivation to study fluctuated according to the different periods of the academic year. The initial excitement at the beginning of each year was followed by a time of discouragement because they were not learning exactly what they wanted and had begun to doubt their ability. Just before the examination period they had to face their fear of failure, which was later replaced by a sense of pride in what they had produced or accomplished. These various feelings were identified as coloring their motivation over the academic year. Although these adults did not question their commitment to their three-year program, their motivation to learn followed an unstable course. Moreover the exact timing of this course was different for each member of the class. Adult educators must be sensitive to the dynamics of this maturation process, willing to talk about it with their students if they think it would be helpful, and willing to let students work out their motivational difficulties as part of the learning process.

Stages of motivation can also be observed throughout the phases of life recorded in students' biographies. Alice, whose narrative was also discussed in Chapter Four, began university right after finishing high school. Because she was not motivated to study, she spent most of her time with other students in social and political groups. She realized when she decided a year or two later after graduation to study in another field that even though she had obtained a degree in literature, she had not really been open to studying in that field when she first started. As she expressed it: "Studying was a pretext for doing something quite different." In her motivational process, learning only in order to pass exams had no interest or meaning for her. Her life experience in a commune and her involvement in the antiwar and the women's liberation movement were the experiences from which she learned something that contributed to her personal growth. Although when she began university again, she admitted that even "in the absence of true intellectual enrichment," her previous study experience was helping her to function in her new academic program.

The maturation of George's motivation to study went through a similar process. After graduating from high school, he chose to go to university to study social science. Very soon he realized, as he said, that he needed to be engaged in a more "real" world. He then chose to work in the field of special education. At the end of his training and after experience in various types of fieldwork, he decided to take a job in a children's home. Ten years later, feeling ready to explore new areas of knowledge, to enlarge his thinking, and to reflect on "the questions arising from his professional experience," he decided to return to the university to get a degree in education.

Paul's educational biography, which I also touched on in Chapter Four, offers another example of a process showing different stages of motivation. After receiving mediocre grades during his school years, he started working at the age of fifteen. As he wanted to find a more interesting job he decided to go to night school to become a technician and later an engineer. The motivation to improve himself and to succeed in the field of his choice entered still another stage in his thirties when he changed his professional orientation entirely by studying psychology and working full time as a yoga instructor.

Adult motivation to learn can be understood both in a sociological and in a psychological context. These two approaches express different aspects of the same reality. In adult learners' narratives, the motivational stages that can be analyzed sociologically very often proceed from what seem to be psychological factors. The influence of family and parental needs is more obvious in early adulthood than it is later in life when the individual has gained more freedom to consider what he or she wants to accomplish. For example, Albert became a florist, as his parents had wished, but then he chose to enter the health profession. The influence of the social environment diminishes as adults become more autonomous. The maturation process results in motivation that belongs more to the realm of the learner. Although uncovering a learner's motivation may take years and cannot be accomplished during the space of a workshop, merely sticking to the established educational program is not a sufficient response from an adult educator. The main role of the adult educator is to empower adults to develop their own motivation to learn, despite the requirements of educational programs.

Transforming the Anonymous World of Education

The educational biographies of adults involved in adult education reveal the distance between education and learning. The dynamics of a life history are not the same as the logic of an organization, even when the organization specializes in education. In students' educational biographies, learning is described as an experience filled with enthusiasm, doubts, and joys. In the world of education, learning is described in terms of programs, objectives, and products.

For the adults who have shared their educational biographies with me, learning belongs to the shaping of their lives and includes multiple aspects of themselves. In the world of education, learning means that the content of the teaching has been assimilated by the student. The warmth of a biographical narrative contrasts with the coldness of a school report. Discovery of one's own needs through a variety of life experiences contrasts with the necessity to adapt to the requirements of an educational program.

At a time when adult education has increasingly become a new period of schooling for many adults, it may be helpful to remind adult education instructors of the difference between the dynamics of learning arising from life experience and the rationality of continuing education programs based on a standardized identification of adult needs. As anyone who has been responsible for teaching adults knows, the main challenge of adult education is student heterogeneity. Most adult education programs are structured as though their participants were homogeneous and, in effect, anonymous. But adults, more than children or teenagers, enter the world of formal education with a variety of expectations and at varying levels in terms of background, motivation, and behavior that are never fully taken into consideration because of fixed norms for achievement and instruction.

When instructors give adult students an opportunity to stop being anonymous and to verbalize the distinctions they find between their expectations and the program requirements, these instructors risk being confronted by students' frustration. When after a certain time my students become less anonymous, it also always becomes harder for me to teach them because I am more aware of the great differences in their backgrounds, motivations, and behaviors. In the same way, it is well known that making students assume a more active role obliges the teacher to be more sensitive to the originality of each contribution. The burden of being absorbed by more personal relationships has been experienced by many educators who have tried to help each participant feel at ease in the context of an educational activity. One of the purposes of helping students understand group dynamics is indeed to make them aware of the difficulties in communicating and decision making when members of a group have different styles, ideas, and attitudes.

Clearly, transforming a group in order to give each of its members the right to find his or her place takes more time than the educational organization allows the instructor. This is probably one reason why a determination to uncover learners' motivations leads some adult educators to choose the workshop format with its more flexible timetable. The time allotted to each activity in continuing education restricts attention to adult motives and forces adult educators to preserve the anonymity of the student in the interest of program efficiency. In continuing education with its emphasis on vocational skills, we are far from the principles of *lifelong education*, which sought to break the bonds of schooling. How is it possible to discover adults' motivations when there is insufficient time to engage in the processes that allow adults to uncover that motivation themselves?

What has been called differential pedagogy offers approaches that can help teachers deal with unequal abilities in a class. It calls for differentiation of teaching to achieve similar educational objectives in different students. It may mean allowing different students different lengths of time for learning before a control test; it may mean using varied types of evaluation. Individualized instruction is another technique used to deal with and preserve the heterogeneity of adult education classes. However, helping adults recognize their individual motivations to learn requires something much more complex than a certain pedagogy. It has to do not only with the organization of education but also with such epistemological questions as: What part of his or her previous education is used by an adult in acquiring new knowledge? Why and how did the individual learn what he or she already knows? Should learning be considered the primary process in becoming an adult? Discussion of these questions is central to marking the boundaries between an educational program organized to achieve its own objectives and an activity that functions in the broader context of adult life.

When I was working as an educational consultant in several agricultural schools, I realized that some of the students who had been learning since childhood to work on farms run by their fathers had no motivation to attend the program largely because it conveyed knowledge they would probably never use. The teachers I worked with had problems maintaining classroom discipline and did not know how to confront students' varied expectations. They asked me to help them find ways to motivate their students to learn. I tried to tell them that the question of motivating these students was not a matter of pedagogy but rather a problem related to the organization of the curriculum in the school and the sociopolitical image of agriculture.

Individualization of the curriculum was too complex to organize and would certainly have cost too much money and time. And, as in many other schools, most of the teachers would have been personally insulted by the idea that a future professional could already know enough in his field even though he had not attended their classes, or did not need to know anything more about their specialized field because his future plans did not require such knowledge. The teachers' image of agriculture had to be maintained as well as the rite of initiation represented by the school years. What was happening in these agricultural schools occurs in most training and is becoming more widespread in adult and continuing education generally. Programs are set up for many reasons other than adult learning, and the result is the low learner motivation faced by instructors. Instructors' naivety about the motivations of their students often comes from the fact that they do not realize to what extent a social order directs the programs for which they work. They want their students to be interested in learning particular things for the sake of those things, whereas the students are there for other reasons, such as pleasing a superior, hoping for a promotion, making a cultural adjustment to a partner, or trying to fulfill a long-time dream.

The perspective of lifelong education as it was developed in the 1960s in international organizations such as UNESCO and the Council of Europe took a much more open view of learning than does the present discourse on continuing education. The need to learn was closely related to the dynamics of social as well as personal life and the context of learning was enlarged far beyond the limits of educational programs. Some of the pioneers who contributed to the principles of lifelong education had an ecological, or systemic, understanding of education. Workplaces, organic communities, and health services were all to be used as an educational environment for enriching the adult learning process. For example, the idea of an "educational district" (Schwartz, 1973) emerged from experiments done with educating the general public in urban areas where a high proportion of people received public assistance and in special housing projects and public health centers. A learning perspective was promoted in which education would make adults increasingly able to take charge of their own lives. How could adult education promote a process of self-education? How could adults be motivated to enrich their own learning processes? These were the kinds of questions raised at the time by adult educators. The educational biography, as an approach centered on adult learning, could help us renew such an approach.

More Educators and Less Andragogy

The time has come for us to question definitions for educators that focus on content. The term *adult educator* still seems to define a general role, but the development of adult and continuing education is leading to a variety of new functions within that role. Adult educators are in charge of the strategy used in an educational activity; they must play leadership roles and may direct evaluations. *Teachers* bear the responsibility for conducting classes for students on the subject matter required by a program. *Instructors* are primarily concerned with transferring attitudes and techniques new to employees and necessary for their efficiency. Titles such as *trainer, tutor, consultant,* and *adviser* may also be used, although the profiles of these functions are hard to define and the training given varies a great deal. Although being an educator has become a profession, people can teach or tutor without knowing much about education. They teach because they are experts in a certain field, or they are asked to be part-time instructors because they have many years of experience in some field and are recognized as being competent. What kind of basic information about education and learning do they need in order to improve the quality of their contribution as adult educators? The same question is relevant for those who play the role of discussion leader, in church groups, for example, or trade union meetings. And what about understanding the general principles of pedagogy or andragogy? How deeply should we go into a discipline such as psychology or sociology when we are asked to contribute to the training of these teachers or instructors? As a university professor involved in the training of trainers, I have discussed these questions with my colleagues time and time again.

One source of answers to these questions and to the issues I have raised in the first part of this chapter is of course educational biography. In the following paragraphs I explain in more concrete terms what I have learned about adult needs, motivations, and dreams from educational biographies, how this knowledge has changed my teaching, and how this same knowledge may help adult educators, whether they are called teachers, instructors, trainers, or advisers, to address the real educational needs of their diverse students.

First, in all encounters with others, the educator is above all a person. Educational biographies show that in adulthood, people remember the teachers they had in school more for themselves than for what they taught. Moreover, people do not remember the personalities of their teachers in isolation as much as they remember the relationship they had with those teachers. It is not the attitudes of the teachers that people describe but rather the influence those attitudes had on their own learning and school experience. A teacher is quoted in an educational biography because he or she made a difficult moment easier or, on the contrary, gave bad grades or was the reason a student dropped out of school. The context of adult and continuing education tends to produce the same social phenomenon: adult students always associate the personalities of teachers with the content of the teachers' courses. When they speak about a workshop or a class they have just attended, adult participants often mention their teachers or trainers. The success of an educational activity depends largely on the teacher. The participants never say that the course content was difficult or that the dynamics of the group were poor without referring to the teacher.

Before deciding to analyze the needs or motivations of their students, adult educators should be aware of their own motivations for teaching or leading a group. They should be clear about their educational goals, their reason for choosing particular techniques, and the place they wish to occupy in the structure of the organization in charge of the program. The best pedagogy will be the one they have designed for themselves, based on a script they like to act because it casts them in the leading role. The best reward will be the enjoyment of being themselves as an invitation to the participants to also be themselves.

Second, continuing one's own education is a condition of being an adult educator. The discipline of making space to be oneself in the context of the personal encounters offered by programs of adult education is more than a single effort made once and for all; it is a continuing process. It is obvious from the educational biographies of experienced adult educators that they have gained their competence through this process. Most of them have not received any formal training but have structured their own professional training by learning what they considered necessary at various times. When they tried to identify the learning process by virtue of which they had gained competence over the years, they mentioned meaningful experiences from the socialization of their younger years, such as being a leader in the Boy or Girl Scouts, or some formal learning activity, such as learning to fly an airplane. The level of schooling did not seem to be an important factor nor did the professional field in which they had specialized. An engineer or a technician did not seem to be less well prepared than someone who had received training in psychology or social work. Nevertheless they had had to include in their process of continuing education whatever they had not learned earlier in life.

It is primarily what educators have done with their education that counts in teaching, together with how they have taken advantage of their former training and experience. Ten years as a secondary school teacher will necessarily lead to competence in areas different from the areas of knowledge produced by ten years as a factory manager. Whatever training they get, adult educators will use their past experience to give it a personal shape.

Third, educational biographies are also full of personal experiences drawn from private life, such as family events that affect relationships, the intercultural experience of moving from one country to another or traveling around the world, or a strong commitment to a religious community. The meaning of these experiences is often understood with the help of knowledge obtained in a workshop or in any kind of specialized program centered on personal development.

The learning due to life experiences and activities of continuing education is closely related to changes in adult life. For adult educators, the need to remain open to life and to construct an autonomous life is the principal motivation for choosing their career and for pursuing their education. They want to maintain the dynamics of change as a learning process, and they want their clients to discover through adult education some real motivation for making meaningful changes in their lives.

Fourth, all adult educators whose educational biographies I have analyzed are questioning the future of their commitment to the profession. They realize that being an adult educator corresponds to a particular stage in their lives, and when they start this job late in life, it is because they have opted for or early retirement from another job or want to move to an occupation in which they can continue to use and expand their existing experience. As adult educators they consider themselves to be on the fringe of the organization for which they work. As I mentioned in Chapter Five, they refer to themselves as "jugglers" or "court jesters" and are very attracted to the idea of keeping a door open to outside influences. For them, learning relates more to the quality of their lives than to the advancement of their careers.

Their educational biographies show very little motivation for a career in adult education. In contrast to schoolteachers, adult educators have held other jobs during their lives, are often part-time or freelance workers, and do not see themselves as being educators for the rest of their lives. They want their status as educators to be recognized, but they also want to be free to drop this status whenever they feel like moving on to some other occupation.

Ideas, Identity, and Convictions

During my adolescence I was very much influenced by adults whom I would call educators even though they were mostly ministers or social workers. I understand today that they were necessary to my development at that time in my life. We are all motivated in our daily cultural behavior by other individuals who are not necessarily educators but who fulfill certain needs of our development. These educators have an influence on the adult learning process not necessarily because they bring interesting ideas but mostly because they offer individuals new ways of being or give an organization a different perspective. Nowadays a majority of adults recognize the credibility of knowledge derived from being and doing. They are no longer interested in discussions of opposing convictions but trust life experiences and consider wisdom a factor of age.

Modern phenomena such as communications media, technology, and publicity are transforming our view of social consciousness. We have a growing tendency to personify political issues and are more disposed to taking a pragmatic position when we consider social change. Being and doing seem to be more important to personal identity than ideas and convictions, and ideas and convictions remain important only when they modify our way of being and our approach to change. At the same time, the anonymity of our cities and our public services, even our clinics and hospitals, has made us more receptive to local traditions of the past and the knowledge that is rooted in the experiences of our ancestors. The popularity of psychological techniques applied to human communication and personal development is, I believe, closely related to our profound need to learn about ourselves and to understand the lives of other people.

Adults are motivated to learn when they feel that the person to whom they are listening or with whom they are working has something to offer because of who he or she is and what he or she is doing. They accept a good teacher, one who knows how to present the content of a course, but they are really motivated to learn in the context of an encounter with a teacher or an instructor who presents a piece of knowledge or introduces a new skill with the authority of life experience. The key pedagogical factors for adult learning are the place, the nature, and the meaning of knowledge within the identity of the educator. The way the educator exposes a theme or presents a skill depends more on who he or she is and what he or she has done than on attractive teaching techniques.

Many teachers and instructors of adults come from social backgrounds differing from those of their students and, in these days of migration, often from different cultures. Literacy programs are a typical example: adult education in these programs becomes a means of cultural socialization for migrants and refugees who need to learn in order to survive in a new society. What could possibly be a more useful pedagogical tool in these instances than educators' awareness of their own motivations to teach and their own convictions about the value of sociocultural integration? When preparing educators, we tend to forget this priority.

Summary

The educational needs of adults have been organized by adult and continuing education practice. These standardized needs tend to reinforce professional, family, and social status and roles. Adults are more and more enrolled in educational activities and less and less aware of what they need as learners.

The interpersonal relationship between learner and adult educator remains a source of motivation. Adults also learn in order to please another person.

Education gives adults space for dreams. Adults expect educational programs to bring changes to their life. Behind their immediate, practical motivation is often an unexpressed level of need that is close to a dream.

The educational biographies of adult educators give us the opportunity to interpret and better understand the process of adult motivation. Many adults need to pass through preparatory stages before choosing what they want to learn.

Educational biographies also help adults discover their needs through interpreting their life experiences, instead of assuming that the requirements of an educational program are the same as their needs.

Being more aware of what they need to learn helps adults in the process of continuing education throughout their lives.

In order to remain sensitive to the needs of their adult students, adult educators should experience being learners and work on the process of identifying their own needs. The biographical approach is therefore a key approach for the training of adult educators.

Chapter Seven

Helping Learners Put Words to Their Lives

Writing educational biographies can enable adults to understand what they have learned through experience. Although this process of putting words to their experiences may produce anxiety, it helps adults to interpret their past learning and guide their future learning.

Pedagogy as a Field of Tradition and Innovation

Most of the time writing is not taken as an objective of adult education. My colleagues consider writing a basic skill that should be acquired by the end of secondary school. Yet in my experience as an adult educator I have always been impressed by the fact that required writing is such a problem for adult learners. As a university professor I noticed that younger students had the same difficulty. For adults young and old, writing a paper is considered a duty and not a way to express personal ideas. Moreover, their drive to do well sometimes leads to anxiety and despair about their ability to write correctly. However, adults with whom I have worked on this issue of resistance to writing have made me realize that it is most often a matter of identity, which has nothing to do with mastering vocabulary or grammar. It is part of what I mentioned earlier in this book as adults' cultural relation to knowledge. These adults have never learned to see themselves as writers. The biographical approach with its oral and written narratives can be an interesting tool with which adult learners can learn to express themselves. It can even play the role of a remedial tool for those who find writing daunting. This chapter suggests several reasons why the educational biography approach may help students with writing to express themselves.

In general, the biographical narrative allows learners to be personal in an academic context. For once they are not obliged to respect a particular style when they write. They can stay away from the models they had to learn at school and instead can have the experience of discovering, by themselves, the right words. Preparing oral and written narratives might transform learners' traditional understanding of taking a public position on the basis of personal experiences or writing a text as a subjective statement.

My experiences of facilitating the writing of educational biographies have been similar with each group. Most of the participants are surprised at how much they enjoy speaking about themselves, sharing personal experiences, and putting together the scattered facets of their life. They also experience real pleasure in finding their own writing style. A written biographical narrative is not a paper they have to write for a university professor. It is not the same as a report or even a personal letter. The narrative does not belong either to the public or the private sphere. Students are also amazed to learn that research can include a subjective side. It somehow contradicts what they have heard about scientific approaches at the university.

Various forms of alternative education have long emphasized the role of oral and written expression. Writing was an important pedagogical tool for the *progressive education* movement in Europe. More recently in the field of adult education, Paulo Freire (1970) called for a *pedagogy of liberation* based on literacy education. Learning to read and write, said Freire, does not have to mean entering the cultural and social world of an oppressive majority. Literacy can and should lead formerly illiterate adults to an expression of their own culture. For Freire, access to language enables adults to put words to a collective experience or a personal condition. Education helps adults give a name to the world. Freire takes a political point of view that values education as action for a more democratic society.

In some ways the biographical narrative can be considered a similar attempt to change the attitudes of adult learners because it helps them put their own words to their learning experiences instead of asking them to adopt the neutral language of the academic culture. Learners have to choose what they want to talk about in the biography. They have to work from their memories, not just answer a questionnaire. They have to unite the emotional and cognitive sides of their expression; maintaining a separation between irrational (emotional) and rational (cognitive) language will not work any more. Relating one's life history orally to a small group might open a new sociolinguistic horizon, and writing a narrative might be a new approach to literary expression. Putting words to the learning experience of a life is formative, a learning experience in itself.

The Task of Interpretation

Most learners in adult education have to face "languages" that they may not have mastered. They speak the languages of the local groups they belong to and frequently feel challenged by the languages used in political, religious, and academic institutions, which tend to be the dominant languages in society. Professionals such as nurses, technicians, and managers have their own languages and tend to interpret the world through the lens of their own vocational culture. Educational biography as a form of expression has to be analyzed in this context. The linguistic styles of the narratives reveal the dependence of adults on social codes, and this knowledge can encourage them to resist that dependence and be creative. In the women's movement the question has often been raised whether there is a feminist way of writing. Though a few women writers have found new styles of writing, we cannot necessarily conclude that there is a women's style of writing. In the same way, it would be an exaggeration to talk about a biographical way of writing, but some of the narratives I have analyzed speak in favor of an attempt to establish a new literary approach that would recognize adults' desire to integrate sensitivity and intellect in their writing style as they interpret their educational experiences.

Students may wish to use nonverbal media in addition to words, and the field of adult education has opened the way to using a number of nonverbal supports to facilitate the expression of emotion among adult groups. These projective techniques, like drawing or collage, were not used in my educational biography seminars, but some researchers have used them in other biographical approaches (Ditisheim, 1984). They give adults an opportunity to deal in a new way with their memories, and they may be particularly useful for adults who do not have the same cultural background as most university students. However, the limits of these techniques and all other techniques of expression must be underlined. Adults will always express themselves in terms of whatever they are able to share. If they are not conscious that an event in their life history has had a real influence on the choices they have made, they will not be able to present it to the group, to socialize it, no matter what tools they have at their disposal. Adult educators are not magicians, and they should be realistic about the means or levels of expression they expect to see. A narrative is therefore the product adults are able to offer in the interpretation of their life history.

Upon hearing about the biographical approach people often have doubts about the meaningfulness of what is shared. Experienced researchers sometimes ask about the truthfulness of the narratives. I always give the same answer. Whatever adults say or write in their narratives has meaning. The very fact that they say it or write it is meaningful. When members of the group ask questions of the narrator, his or her answers continue to follow the limits of what he or she is able to share. The narratives belong to the *world of interpretation*. The process of constructing the narratives is a process of interpretation. Adult learners work on their pasts and try to find the right words to express their learning or formative experiences. If an interpretation were to be forced, it might not express what the person really means. This happens when people answer questionnaires, for instance; they force themselves to answer a question that they have not raised for themselves.

Words Versus Scientific Data

The emotional content of the oral presentation and the literary dimension of the written presentation give biographical narratives a special status. The text has to be interpreted as a whole and is destroyed when reduced to categories of analysis. The data collected can be considered witnesses. Analysis can be understood as a dialogue more than as a systematic attempt to count tendencies. Because everything about the biographical narrative imposes qualitative data on the researcher, it does not make much sense to oppose the qualitative methodology and favor the quantitative.

Educational biography produces information that interprets an individual's learning experiences; therefore it leaves much space and time uncovered. The data that are revealed have to be seen as footprints or fragments of an adult's life. It does not matter that the biography as it is told is full of gaps and holes. The words used name life experiences that led to learning, shaping an educational biography. The words are the signs, the data that tell us what adults want to say about their learning. There is no system we can apply to understand a biography. We have to trace what each learner knows about his or her learning experiences through the words he or she has chosen to describe them.

Furthermore, adults adapt their narratives to the group in which they are working. They are, as I said, in a dialogue. They would use different words with different participants. As Ferrarotti (1983) has said: "The forms and the content of a biographical narrative differ according to the people to whom they are addressed. They depend on the interaction in the social area of communication" (p. 52; my translation). Therefore the style of the narrative also reflects the style of the group to which it is presented. And the value of the narrative will depend partly on the quality of listening and understanding that exists in the group. This is why it is important that adult learners spend enough time in their groups to develop a group climate and build the quality of the dialogue.

It is also important for adult learners to have a reasonable length of time to work on the quality of their narratives. Whatever the life history, the narrative develops and matures during the time spent thinking about it, remembering the past, selecting what is really meaningful, and finding the words for the final, written version. This is why in my seminars we take the stages of preparation seriously and we value the time allowed between the oral and written versions. There are, nevertheless, limits to any methodology. The narratives remain dependent on some degree of self-reflection done by each adult before his or her educational biography is started.

One way to assist students in understanding that words are their data and that the biography is a process of interpretation is to use the teacher's own educational biography as an example. In my research team, we have given our educational biography groups our own narratives, although another question we have had to resolve is whether to use the same narratives repeatedly or to revise them. The solution I have usually adopted is to give the group the last written version of my narrative before they start writing. On other occasions, however, I have chosen to give only an oral version, which thus had its meaning in the context of the group. I clearly explained that my narrative was not a model that had to be followed and that it could develop and mature over different versions, which had an impact on their understanding of the seriousness of the methodology. In this way I provided qualitative criteria to help pave the way for their own products.

Finding the Meaning of Experiential Learning

What is asked of the students at the time they have to present the formative side of their life history is to be explicit about their experiential learning. They do not describe the content of their formal school learning, but they try to explain how school and other life events and relationships have influenced and directed their experiences of learning. They select wording that reflects their interpretation, a process that is not easy for most adults, who are more inclined to describe the outer shape of an experience than to explore its inner meaning. This problem in writing also exists for many adult educators when they are asked to share not just descriptions of but the meanings of interesting experiences they have had in working with adults.

Today, guidance counseling intended to help adult students assess their experiential learning in order to possibly obtain some academic credit for it also has the effect of helping adults give words and meaning to their life experiences. The learning side of an experience has to be explained before that experience can be assessed in terms of learning, and this explanation process benefits students in some of the same ways that educational biography does. Some adult students are asked to prepare portfolios of their achievements for assessment, and one of the items in these portfolios may be a written general picture of their education throughout their lives. They might even be asked to produce an autobiography (Robin, 1992).

Adult learners may also have to assess their learning as part of a particular program. They may have to identify what they already know and how they will learn the part of the program that is new to them. As the use of computer technology becomes commonplace, students will have to become more self-directed in their learning, and this too will require them to have reflected deeply on their learning experiences and their current needs. Adult educators must become aware that part of their teaching responsibility is to allow time to discover what the different adult members of a group already know and what they want to learn. As I have said many times, the projected content of a program carries no learning guarantee. If they want to plan their own program based on the general program offered, adult learners have to be aware of what they already know and what they want to learn. Helping them find the words to make their position explicit should be part of any formal learning process.

The need to assess experiential learning has been an important reason for including counseling in the work of adult and continuing education. The biographical approach can be an instrument for helping adults assess what they know and clarify what they want to learn. Indeed, educational biography has played this role for some of the students with whom I have worked. For example, I remember a woman who, after examining the entire course of her life during the seminar, came to the realization that the time had come for her to leave teaching and start working in a new direction.

One further thing has to be stressed here. The requirement to put words to life and learning experiences requires in turn a real commitment on the part of the learner. The meaning of experiential learning relates to the whole process of an individual's experience. Adult learners have to set explicit criteria, a rationale, for selecting those experiences that are learning experiences. The rationale they use opens the way to a possible language for or a possible socialization of their experience. This task of being explicit about learning experiences takes time. Finding the right word takes time. Explicit meaning is the result of a process that seems to have no shortcuts. The search for instruments to simplify the biographical approach now that assessment of experiential learning and formal assessment centers are becoming more common might result in processes that impose standards for life experiences or norms for valuing experiential learning. That is, the criteria for selecting and discussing learning experiences might be set by others, not by the individual learners. We must remember that putting their own words to their own life experiences is a necessary step for learners in the process of recognizing an experience as a learning experience and extracting its meaning.

Writing as a Cause of Anxiety

Writing, which is an almost daily responsibility for a scholar at the university, makes most adult students anxious, and an examination of the reasons may tell us something about writing anxiety among adult learners in general. Educators involved in working or teaching with adults have difficulty with writing, and when they have an opportunity to publish or when they become the students as they continue their own education, they often refuse to write about their diverse and multiple experiences. It is sometimes a question of time. But in addition, writing and working, like reflection and action, do not seem to them to belong to the same rationale. The mental distance required and the formal rules of writing to be followed do not seem natural to active adult educators. They are not comfortable with the idea of taking a pause, looking back at something that belongs to the past. Thus adult educators tend to disqualify their ability to write and find excuses not to do it. When they finally do decide to publish an article, they often feel ashamed of the final product.

In our research centered on the construction of professional competency among adult educators, the adult educators of the second research group refused to write even their educational biographies. They did not feel the need to deepen their narratives by preparing a more formal version once they had completed the oral version. The reasons for this refusal were multiple. I understood it as a sign that they saw themselves mainly as participants in the research my colleagues and I were doing and that they did not see themselves as researchers into their own lives. They wanted to explore our life history approach and were open to talking about the content of the oral narratives. They were also interested in the possible applications they might make of educational biography in their own teaching, but they were not committed to a reflection dealing with adult educators' general competency. This experience made me aware that the obstacles adults see when they are asked to write may arise in the first place because the adults have not understood the meaning of what they are asked to do. For example, the difficulty and often the delay that characterize the production of a thesis or a doctoral dissertation at a university reveals to me the lack of relevance this type of product has for most students. Conversely, when adults are expressing themselves to others by writing about their own experiences, they either find the right words promptly or accept the challenge to find the right words. But if the social dimension of writing is not obvious to most adult educators, why would they write themselves? They do not necessarily take the time to read the literature in their field, and if they do, they do not necessarily enjoy it or benefit from the time they have spent. Consequently, why would they publish in order to contribute to this activity they do not take seriously?

The value of making the effort to use the right words to describe an experience is apparent to adults when they are searching for the meaning of their experiences or feel the necessity to reflect on them. The narratives that seem most meaningful for the reader are the ones in which the style of writing shows that the author is deeply expressing himself or herself and is not merely responding to a request to write. This is important for biographical work at the university level. Most university exams request written responses. A written narrative of some kind can therefore be taken as a normal academic requirement. However, when a narrative asks students to work on key questions of their own biography, writing should play a different role. The thin boundary between these two ways of writing and of understanding the meaning of a written text marks a difference to which the person responsible for facilitating the biographical approach should be very sensitive, in order to convey that distinction to his or her students. This is why, after ten years of research, I am still looking for new ways to help adults improve the written version of their narratives. New technologies might play a role, as has been the case for recent written narratives in my seminars. Technology has enabled some students to include schemes, drawings, and even photographs in order to produce a new style of written narrative.

It could also be helpful to encourage students to prepare a second or even a third version of their narratives if they are open to growing more comfortable with writing and to extending their research. This extension might take different forms. In a few experiments my colleagues and I have made with small groups, some students prepared new versions of their biographies in order to deal with the construction of a specific aspect of learning. That is, they narrowed the focus of the narrative. Some students have also been interested in revisiting and rethinking their narratives after a space of a year or two from the original writing.

An Epistemological Question and a Position

There are of course epistemological questions arising from the practice of writing when writing itself is a way of knowing. Why are some adults happy to write when others are nervous about any text they have to produce? What does this mean in term of their own identity, their relationship to knowledge? Is writing the best way for reflecting upon life experiences, or should we imagine different methods for knowing in this instance? Why do different people use different styles in putting words to life experiences? Is there a relationship between schooling and writing ability, or is the ability to write dependent on other factors? Why does one woman say in the middle of her narrative, "I look at the world through words. I have a vital need to write and to read," whereas another resists preparing a written version even though she greatly enjoyed the oral one?

The task of writing an educational biography presents a good opportunity for students to discuss the practice of writing and the epistemological issues it raises. For one thing, such discussion may help them become more sensitive to the various styles of learning among adult learners. In the school tradition we all learned to write according to models and under pressure. Now students may come to respect the time needed for the production of a matured and reflective text in a style the writer has chosen. And they may also learn that the final version remains limited by the words an individual is able to put to his or her life history. The approach is not a matter of getting the best narrative possible but of getting the best educational version possible of a life history.

The questions about ways of knowing raised by the life history approach are also shedding new light on the production of knowledge. If I emphasize the research side of the educational biography, it is because I am convinced that in this approach, each student can play the role of a researcher. If a life history is the resource material required for research centered on adult processes of learning, then specific questions about a specific life history have to be identified by the author-researcher himself or herself. The words an individual uses to describe his or her personal experiences have a singular meaning that belongs to the author. Educational biography is a means of sharing these singular experiences in a group, with language as the social tool that allows this sharing. This has to be emphasized. As Ferrarotti (1983) has so well expressed it: "What makes an act or an individual history unique has to be considered a possible path to scientific knowledge of a social system" (p. 51; my translation). In other words, being subjective is a way to be scientific. In our difficulties with writing to express our experiences, we are paying for the empirical tradition in the various disciplines of human science. We are the victims of the hierarchical stratification of scientific knowledge. Nurses, for example, do not feel authorized to write about their clinical experience because the dominant model of scientific research in medicine has a quantitative focus. We are also influenced by our common understanding of social history, which most of the time portrays not simple lives but the lives of the more glamorous historical figures. Yet each of us is embedded in social history, and most of the biographies I have collected show how a single life history takes place in a broader social context. The personal side cannot be divided from its social dimension. As one adult learner comments: "I know, because I have felt it, that I have been caught in a family, social, and cultural history from which I have slowly taken a distance without being able to avoid keeping it at the soles of my shoes. Memories of my body, the wandering of my soul, where the life of my narrative takes place." Most of the written biographies I have read are testimonies of both a singular life and a period of history and, as Alheit has often written, combine structure and subjectivity.

When I refer to the uniqueness of each life history, I do not of course mean that one narrative is enough to define the process of adult learning. As I described earlier, single narratives contribute to a hypothesis about adult learning when their meanings resonate across multiple narratives from different students. That is, the hypothesis is not proven but confirmed. Some authors, as I discussed in Chapter Two, have taken another position. Rather than gather meanings from multiple biographies they deepen their theoretical analysis of a single life history (Pineau and Marie-Michèle, 1983; Catani, 1973; Catani and Mazé, 1982). However, for me, interpretation arises out of the interaction that takes place in the dialogue of the educational biography group and in the implicit dialogue between all the biographies the researcher has in mind from his or her reading.

A Path Between the Ephemeral and the Essential

In our present world, word and text have become part of the cultural market. The value of a book depends more on its marketplace popularity than on its contents. Moreover, the multiplicity of messages we now receive is having a tendency to diminish the meaning of all that is said or written and to foster a generalized impression of confusion, which is reinforced by the difficulty of distinguishing different styles of information. The media have changed our sense of time in the understanding of messages.

In this context of what is popularly called "information overload," the question of the social image and social importance of the life history approach has to be raised. Biography as a literary style has a cultural patrimony of glorious autobiographies as well as the more vulgar world of tabloid journalism. Compared to such products, educational biography can be characterized by its search for meaning. Again, it belongs to the world of interpretation, and the criterion for assessing its impact is not the attention given to it but the authenticity of its content. People sometimes say that biography is a mood. I doubt that the biographical approach presented here will ever fall into this trap. The commitment it requires will prevent it from becoming simply a game adults enjoy playing.

During the current period of social change, the life history approach might also be a way of putting words to one's social and cultural heritage. By presenting their educational biographies, adults are also presenting a variety of social and cultural worlds, the values they have known in the past and the ones they are carrying with them into the future. I believe that the life history approach might be a way to keep alive those cultural heritages that have utility for our present society. This approach is therefore a way to transform the past into resources for the present. For example, a group of Protestant theologians working with young people who are doing apprenticeships or looking for jobs have constructed a project in which the value of work as it has shaped the lives of retired people can be compared with the ideas these young people have about their vocational lives. The biographical narratives of retired workers will be the vehicle for this dialogue.

I also see the life history approach as a way to fight a widespread tendency to use adult education to meet mostly people's ephemeral needs, to treat it as a "just in time" methodology. The emphasis in educational biographies on each adult's finding his or her own words may be a way to hold the line against the homogeneous codes that are coming to dominate the cultural market, to counter the standardization of language. The media and the new information technologies are largely imposing symbolic behaviors on the younger generations. The media have, for example, reduced the worlds of sports, music, and politics to images of the winners or the most commercially successful in each field. Today adults encounter cultural references that are mostly dominated by the models of others. The media focus on movie stars and "heroes" and, at the opposite extreme, on social victims establishes a world of symbols, and most people then try to find an identity for themselves out of the materials of this artificial world. In contrast, learning to use their own words becomes a way for adults to work on building their own identities out of their own life histories. This is true for many techniques of personal development. The educational practice of educational biography belongs to the movement in adult education that values creative expression and that leads to more personal language.

A recent idea in adult education is to promote what we call in French *pedagogie du projet* (pedagogy project). It is a way to build a life plan for oneself or an educational plan for a professional team. Educational biography could be a complement to the same movement. Looking at the past, checking roots, and giving names to experiential learning help adults clarify the future they want to build. Helping adults to identify a life project has become the main objective of several European workshops and some counseling efforts. In order to speak about a life project or to write about it, adults must appropriate their lives, take possession of them. This is a more social side of the use of life history in adult education, and it is closely related to working and professional life.

Freire (1970) has clearly explained how literacy should result in the ability to express one's own culture, not conformity to the dominant culture and mastery of only the language of others. We see both in adult education. In the case of conformity, we see that good students who have always been able to turn in excellent academic papers are often paralyzed when they have to find their own words for writing about something they have experienced. Secondary school teachers are typical examples of adults who face plenty of difficulties finding their own words for a narrative about their professional practice.

The personalization of speaking and writing goes together with its socialization. This may be one important source of the power of the educational biography. It is also a key point for adult learning. The objectives of adult education programs very seldom combine the needs of individuals' personal and professional lives. This sort of splitting in most people's lives has been reinforced by the systems of interpretation they have been using for understanding the reality of their lives. Sometimes psychology is on one side, and politics is on the other. In Europe it has often been Freud on one side and Marx on the other. Religious interpretations often oppose an inner life to a life of social involvement. Typically, at different biographical stages adults will have used different systems of this type and these systems' concomitant languages to understand their lives. But these systems have become more and more outdated and meaningless. Therapy has helped some adults to better understand who they are. Commitment to social and political action has helped some realize the struggles of any society. In the present economic crisis, we are facing new challenges. We are searching for cultural values and spiritual convictions that may help us answer all our open questions. The methodology of life history is certainly not a miracle solution, but it should be seen in this broad perspective. Education finds here its basic meaning, which is to lead people from a former place to a new place. Educational biography is a methodology that can help students find the words to describe their lives and experiences as part of preparing for and undergoing this change. In our present world it also gives the field of adult education a new perspective. Beyond the responsibility to transmit a cultural heritage and to teach the languages of the past, education has always had the goal of fighting obsolete knowledge and providing the necessary qualifications to the new generation. Scientific and technological knowledge have been educational priorities for years. Now we may be entering a new era in which culture has to play a more central role. Helping adults find the right words to explain their life histories, what they have learned throughout their lives, and what is important for them in regard to the future might be a vital trend in the education of adults.

Summary

Although oral and written expression is considered a basic skill, most students face difficulty when they have to find their own words to express themselves. The biographical approach might facilitate literary expression and become a learning experience in itself.

Progressive pedagogy and progressive educators always stress personal expression as a tool of emancipation. Freire opened a perspective on illiteracy that should be taken seriously for literate adults as well. Language is a vehicle of communication necessary for any social thought.

A biographical narrative finds its final version through an interpretive process. It needs time and reflective thought. For weeks, students listen to and discuss oral narratives and work on their own. In a way, each person tells himself or herself various life histories before finding the one he or she wants to address to the group. In introducing their written versions, students often mention how they did their work on these narratives and the difficulties they have had.

Experiential learning has become a subject of assessment in adult education. This helps adult learners become used to putting words to their learning experiences. Being explicit about what they have learned in the course of their personal or professional lives should become a regular practice for learners and educators in the field of adult and continuing education.

Biographical narratives may open new epistemological perspectives on ways of knowing. Examining the meaning of a singular life in order to suggest a hypothesis about adult learning is far from the traditional practice of the human sciences. However, in the biographical narrative, knowledge implies subjectivity. For me as an adult educator, the subjectivity of educational biography is a way to make learning as it takes place the locus of research.

Chapter Eight

Giving Evaluation Another Meaning

Evaluation is the field of research that helped me discover the biographical dimension of adult learning. It was also through the practice of evaluation that I came to understand the meaning of having adults be participants in the process of research. This understanding began when, in the process of researching and writing my dissertation, I was using an empirical approach to evaluation, collecting data that were supposed to verify the outcomes of a program of continuing education.

This chapter, then, does not consider evaluation of educational biography but represents an attempt to go back to my previous scientific concern with a new perspective. It presents some exploratory research that I conducted that attempted to discover the process that was the key element for understanding adult learning. Later, I also tried to transfer my experience of educational biography to a more instrumental domain in the field of education. At the time each objective was a personal challenge. In the process of discussing this research, the chapter reinforces many of the points I have been making about the essential role educational biography can play in adult learning.

These exploratory pieces of research should also be understood by adult educators as an inspiring way of conducting research. This chapter is therefore an invitation for them to use evaluation as an opportunity to analyze the processes through which adult learning takes place and not only as a methodology for controlling the products of teaching. It is also a way to include research in the process of teaching and to reflect with the students themselves on adult learning.

Finally, rather than describe this research in chronological order, I look first at the research that allowed me to try to incorporate educational biography methodology into evaluation and that added considerably to my own understanding of adult learning, showing the potential of expanding our ideas about evaluation. Then I discuss my earlier research in identifying processes of learning.

How to Evaluate a Training Program for Adult Educators

Many years ago I began to address the question of how to evaluate a training program for adults. Since then I have discovered the biographical approach and led many groups in preparing educational biographies. After reading the first book I wrote on educational biography (Dominicé, 1990) and becoming interested in the views I had developed on adult processes of learning after reading learners' educational biographies, a French university professor invited me to be in charge of the evaluation of an adult educator training program sponsored by a group of firms in Paris. I considered this offer an occasion to attempt a transfer of the biographical approach into the practice of evaluation.

The program I had to evaluate was organized around six main topics that were covered during three days of lectures, group workshops, and field trips. The professor described what he expected from the evaluation in a very clear way: the evaluation required descriptive and reflective attention to the process of learning. Trainees should reconstitute their process of learning, mention by name its different stages, its nature, and the various connections involved. My colleague did not want an evaluation intended to control the effectiveness of the program but one that assessed the program's impact on the participants. He expected the participants to be explicit about the types of learning they could attribute to the program. The work he knew I had done on life history was, according to him, appropriate to the evaluation of such a training program. He wanted the evaluation to be part of the program and the participants to realize what and how they had learned from this program. It was for him a good way to understand the processes of learning that might characterize adult learning in this kind of program.

This evaluation was done with three different groups over a period of four years. I have had about four days each time, one day at the beginning and one at the end with the group of about twelve adult educators and two days for personal interviews in between. The first day I gave a brief introduction about the direction the evaluation would take. Later I worked with the learners on the structure of the evaluation and the reason for its different parts. The objective of the first day was to encourage the learners' investment in this evaluation as a kind of exploratory research project in which everybody would adopt the research objectives set by the program organizers. Each group of educators showed a real interest in this new orientation for an evaluation, but at the end of each program, employed as they were in multinational corporations such as IBM and Digital Equipment Corporation, they were overwhelmed by the weight of their other responsibilities. They had difficulty saving time for something not immediately useful. Even when the dates of the interviews were decided long before they took place, learners often apologized for not having had the time to prepare for them. Some of them never submitted the written portion of the evaluation I asked them to produce. Adult educators are facing real conflicts when they try to find time for reflection on the processes of learning they observe in their adult students. The logic of action is not the same as the logic of research. The planning of programs is always, according to adult educators, taken more seriously than the dynamics of adult learning.

After this introduction, I asked the learners to prepare for the meeting I had planned with each of them. These interviews were semidirective, structured around the themes I had discussed with them during the first day: their needs, the plan of the program, the interaction between the effects of the program and their life histories, the nature of the knowledge and learning at stake, and their expectations for follow-up. They were not obliged to deal with each of these points, but they knew that our discussion would take place around these themes.

The first year I asked them to go through all the course material and notes they had, and I suggested that to summarize the impact of the program, they draw something representing their final view of the dynamics of the program. Only two or three of them did this. I concluded that they had too many difficulties adapting to this projective approach, and I finally dropped it. After seeing every participant in an interview of at least one hour, I went back to the whole group for a final day with a new request. On the basis of the feedback I had given them, they had to select some common key themes or questions they wanted to discuss more deeply. My feedback was structured on the notes I had from the interviews. With these notes I had tried to read the interviews after hearing them, in a kind of biographical perspective. In other words I came back to the participants at the end with two approaches for evaluating the learning process: one related to the main themes they had shared in their interviews and could now analyze more deeply, and the second related to their individual understanding of the meaning for their specific life history of what they had learned in the program. After this final day they were expected to produce a narrative describing their own learning process, and I had committed myself to write another text based on the common key themes. This method of evaluation turned out to be very stimulating but too costly in time to realize fully. The second and third years I did this evaluation, I had to simplify it and provide feedback on all the interviews with a few common points to be discussed with the participants and later on with the professor in charge of the program.

My idea had been to combine the two different dimensions of the individual and the group and I had thought that everyone would take seriously all the work implied by this type of evaluation. My expectations were again too high. I now understood better why the practice of evaluation has received more technical than theoretical support. From a researcher's point of view, evaluation has to be simplified in order to produce some immediate results. I was nevertheless disappointed by the participants who did not find time for a final written narrative about the contribution of the program to their learning process. I remain convinced that such an evaluation is a key stepping-stone for adults if they are to reach an understanding of their ways of learning and to contribute to a research process about adult learning.

Adult learners are typically more eager to obtain a certificate than to reflect on their learning process, even when this reflection is included in the program. Yet this kind of evaluation could bring much to the understanding of adult learning. Here are three examples of concepts from the evaluations of this adult educators' course that have contributed to my own understanding of the question of adult learning.

For many participants the person who was in charge of the program became a figure they identified with. They did not want him to be a model, but they recognized his way of acting in the group and of dealing with theoretical issues as a reference for their own responsibility. In other words the leader of the group became a central influence in shaping the participants' professional identity as adult educators. One woman told me, "He legitimates every part of what I do." She added that "the job of adult educator requires a strong professional identity. I should also be an example to my students; it is an important part of my responsibility as an adult educator." For another participant, the leader was a facilitator of learning: "His way of explaining the themes we have discussed gave me an opportunity to feel able and clever." This could mean that the capacity to engage in one's own way of thinking is aided by the opportunity to think along with another person or to be recognized by him or her. In addition, identification was extended to the specialist resource persons involved with the program, so that identification seemed to be a general principle of learning. It appeared that the participants learned because of a person they had heard, met, or worked with in the program. This attitude was a confirmation of what I had heard in most educational biographies when adults spoke about their schooling. Learning is, most of the time, related to the student's personal relationship with the teacher.

In this program I also saw that this principle has a counter-effect. In the remaining two sessions of the program, a number of participants rejected the same leader because they did not feel recognized by him. They were critical and held him responsible for the work they had and had not done. They rejected him because they felt rejected by him. This confirms how much the dynamics of learning for adults who have to open themselves to new fields of study or to new ways of thinking depend on the quality of their relationship with the adult educator.

In a training program it is not always easy to differentiate between learning that belongs to new knowledge and behavior and learning coming out of one's own explanation of life and existing professional experiences. For some experienced adult educators, a training program they take themselves might be an opportunity to make their own experiences meaningful. As one woman commented on the program: "I consider that I was qualified enough before the program started, but I was afraid to make use of qualifications which were not validated." That is, she knew she had these qualifications as a result of her vocational experience, but without certification she did not fully trust them. Evaluation is often a way for adults to recognize their experiential learning. This kind of evaluation should be heard as a real challenge. Because of her vocational experience, this woman did not need to be trained. What she did need was help in recognizing what she already knew. She adds something even more challenging: "Educators with experience do not know. They have to be careful not to refer to their experience if they want to show that they know." What she means is that in the face of the formal knowledge of the adult educators who have university backgrounds and are able to master academic language and theories, the educators who have gained their competency mainly from experience are afraid to show that they know too. For many participants, then, this program was a way of gaining a language or a theoretical support for presenting their experience. Before the program started, as one of them says, they were "doing things without knowing that they were doing them." Self-learning processes are not recognized unless they can be certified.

The main challenge for a group with participants from various institutions comes from the diversity of contexts. Such a group obliges everyone in it to depart from the perspective of his or her daily routine. Participants have to listen to different problems, presented with different logic or in the light of different organizational settings. What has impressed me the most is how much adult educators adapt themselves to the local culture in which they work. If they came from an engineering firm, they understood learning from a technical point of view. They worked as technicians and became trainers because of their interest in training engineers or because they were recognized as being able to take on this type of responsibility. They stayed in their familiar cultures, and so when they came to a program like the one I evaluated, they discovered a new field. Some of them were very enthusiastic and opened themselves to the new dimensions of communications or group dynamics. For adult educators with social science backgrounds the reaction was quite different. They enjoyed other participants' experiences. The program gave them the opportunity to apply their frame of reference to a new reality. These encounters between local cultures justify organizing a training program for adult educators from multiple companies. Learning is related to the capacity to be open to new points of view and to move out of old frames of reference. Often playing the role of mediator, adult educators have to learn to be flexible about theory. That is one of the main goals of an adult educator training program.

How Students Develop Their Intellectual Itineraries

Some years before I conducted the evaluation work with this training program, I had explored another approach. In a course titled "Evaluation and Adult Education," I wanted students to have an opportunity to experiment with the way a nontraditional approach to evaluation could lead to a research process. I suggested they work on their university itineraries, their overall course schedules, treating their time as higher education students as a biographical phase. They were all working toward a degree in education and were taking as many units as possible in the time available to them given their other commitments to jobs, families, and so forth. The object of research was to identify their process of learning as it had taken place so far in the degree program they were following. This curriculum contained a number of required courses as well as optional courses. Students usually enrolled in the course on evaluation at the end of the curriculum, namely in their third or fourth year at university.

I asked the students to form several small groups, and then, working within one of these groups, each student was asked to follow a scheme with the following steps:

First, the student made a list, the itinerary, of each course and seminar taken each year.

Second, in an exchange with the group, the student gave reasons for his or her choice of courses and the structure of the itinerary followed. Each group then shared with the other groups a summary of the group members' reasons for choosing certain courses.

Third, on the basis of the list of courses and reasons for the choices made, each student found a way to define what he or she considered he or she had learned in each one. This definition was intended to give students an idea of the type of knowledge and learning concerned.

Fourth, instead of counting the effects of the different courses, each student was to find a drawing that represented the processes involved with the identified learnings. Students shared their drawings with the small group and then with the total group.

This evaluation required collecting data and working on an interpretation. I was careful not to ask students to discuss the value of the different courses, which would have put me in trouble with my colleagues. I underlined the necessity of focusing on their own approach to the degree program and their own behavior in the learning process. The purpose of the evaluation was not to assess the quality of the program but the interaction between the program and the student in terms of its impact on each student's learning processes. I have always been impressed by the many hours spent by teachers on curriculum. They try again and again to decide on the right structure for conveying the content of a program or the structure that will be the most helpful for the students. They want students to learn in what the teacher considers the right way, but as all of us in education know, the logic of the teacher is not the same as the logic of the learner. For once I wanted to discover something about the logic of the learner.

The results were quite instructive. First of all, the students did not organize their individual curricula according to a simple logic of learning. Instead, they tried to satisfy a variety of needs: to meet the requirements of the degree program itself, to find some relevance to their present jobs, to satisfy their curiosity as learners who had often not had a traditional schooling, to fulfill the expectations of their employers, and perhaps even to attend class at a certain time of day or along with a friend or a colleague. These needs do not have much to do with the criteria followed by the organization in designing the overall program curriculum. In other words, the structure of the program did not match up with the reasons students chose a course.

The learning students mentioned and their explanations of the nature of this learning were also certainly different from the organization's and the teachers' declared objectives. Paradoxes were not absent from these shared observations. Some students who hated one course had emphasized its impact, not because of its planned content but because their lack of interest in that content had forced them to devise a different content by themselves. Students mentioned learning in relation to different facets of knowledge, and some of their drawings showed these differences. One group used the image of a cake with pieces of different flavors. A course might, for instance, relate more to one's previous knowledge, philosophical options, or vocational future. This content might have been meaningful or not depending not on its subject but on the way it was organized or presented. Specific rules were apparent in each case. Learning might arise from a lack of knowledge about and previous training in the content or, to the contrary, from an interest structured by years of studying similar themes. In the same way, professional responsibility might explain learning that was directly related to the one's field or that belonged to a totally different but useful field. Students have needs and dreams, as I have said. They adopt tactics and are logical according to their own criteria. At the same time, they may be afraid to be autonomous in their approach to learning because they know they must pass a test or they carry doubts about their knowledge.

These students' motivation varied over time, a phenomenon I mentioned in an earlier chapter. Enthusiasm was more evident at the beginning or at the very end of the program. They had phases of discouragement in between. For adult students who are attending university classes for the first time in their lives, the beginning of study is a time of anxiety. They often initially choose classes where they have little to learn so they know they will not fail. Some drawings used spirals to illustrate the obstacles overcome by the learner during a course of study. Other drawings pointed to the conflicts faced—for example, between the necessity of following a rule and the willingness to be creative.

In the comments they made about this exploration, students underlined how new it was for them to analyze their learning behavior and to use evaluation in such a comprehensive way. Instead of using evaluation to control a product, they had used it for understanding processes. It put the results of the program in another light for them. Learning now appeared as a process full of complexity, and the final question was more how to respect the way adults learn in a program than how to make them learn the content of a teaching unit.

How Students Learn

Some years after, I understood why the emphasis had to be put on the process and not the product in order to understand the transformations in adult behavior due to learning. I conducted the first experiment in my own classroom. I asked approximately sixty students in an introductory course in adult education to fill out a questionnaire based on statements derived from empirical observations over the years about students' ways of learning. (In all, my assistant and I created three different instruments, one for each trimester.) The students were free to use the instrument as they wanted. The statements were intended to be supports or stimuli for the expression of the students' own reactions and commentaries, and the students were invited to use the instrument as a guideline for writing a kind of diary. Here are some examples of the statements to which students were asked to react: "The uncertainty of the first weeks is difficult to go through"; "If the future of my job was clear, this course would take on another meaning"; "Adults retain the learning style they built during their school years." Students responded to some statements more than others. Most of them did not find it easy to share their reactions—first, because they were not used to observing themselves as learners but also because they did not fully trust that there would be no negative result from their comments. I nevertheless collected many interesting data.

This research has opened the door to a better understanding of the diversity means of self-regulation that govern learning in formal education. In this adult educators' class, the syllabus is not formalized. The content is constructed through collective reflection and the discussion of experiential learning. The students have the opportunity to participate and share ideas from their own experiences as educators. They are not asked to memorize the content of the teaching, but they are invited to a learning process that might involve a personal or even biographical dynamic. This research has helped the students and me identify what type of self-regulation resulted from attending the course. In other words, the students' learning was analyzed as a process of the rules the students applied not so much to the content but to the ways they interacted with academic knowledge as it was presented and discussed.

After the students and I had analyzed the data in several ways, the following four ideas emerged. One student comment illustrates each point.

First, the learners' life history, especially the impact of their school years, shaped their image of themselves as students, and their attitudes toward knowledge also related to their professional experiences. One student reported, for example: "I need to think, to learn, to fill myself again and I fear going beyond myself."

Second, the group of students provided a place of dialogue, a source of enrichment through exposure to different life and job experiences, and a reinforcement of common interests. Another student found, for example, that "the group is a big help for the answer I am looking for."

Third, the themes of the lectures introduced a world of ideas and reflection and suggested an approach for working on the questions raised. One student said, for example, that "the course made me realize the different aspects of adult education and the challenge of continuing education for our societies. I had no idea of the complexity of this domain."

Fourth, the oral contributions they made in the class and the papers they wrote deepened the meaning of the theoretical work for the students. As one of them stated, "Writing is an important support for clarifying my ideas."

Learning as a formative process reflected implicit rules related to these four ideas. This general dynamic could be the focus of evaluation centered on learning. The content of teaching is formative as long as it clarifies the ways students learn and look at themselves as learners. For the training of adult educators in particular, I believe it is important to offer this opportunity of combining teaching and learning. If the task of evaluation is oriented toward an understanding of learning processes, the attitude toward evaluation will change. Instead of feeling controlled by the norms implied in the evaluation, students will contribute through their participation in the evaluation process to the production of the knowledge they will need as adult educators. Given this perspective, evaluation might take the form of exploratory research.

Evaluation as an Exercise of Power

What I heard in students' biographical narratives about evaluation reinforced my position. Evaluation plays a key role in adults' memories of school. Being subject to evaluation has often structured their attitudes toward formal learning in a way that persists into their adult years. One woman expressed herself very strongly on this matter: "There is a failure in my school record which has troubled my relation with myself. I will never forget this failure: it bothers my decisions and restrains my boldness. If I want to forget this bad memory I should, I believe, fight for my high school degree and therefore find proof that I am able to obtain it." If evaluation were the focus of adults' educational biographies, those biographies would often reveal a world of wounds collected throughout people's schooling and remaining vivid later in life.

For many adults the school grading system has nourished their doubts about themselves. Grades are very often taken as more than an indicator of what has been learned. Grades and diplomas earned during their school years seem to give adults their identities as learners. They serve as a test qualifying the level of what people can learn. Adults who were mediocre students have continuing doubts about their capacity to learn unless they obtain better grades in their adult learning. It is not so much the grades as such that cause these severe personal judgments but the interpretation given to school grades by the social environment and the learners themselves. This is why adult and continuing education can have a remedial side for adult learners.

There is a parallel between the way I moved from the categories of adult development to the biographical understanding of adult life and the way I moved from measuring the effects of a program to searching for the meaning learners attribute to the various times or stages of their formal education. Evaluation has been an important part of the scientific work done in the field of education in the last twenty years, yet on the basis of what I have heard in students' biographical narratives, I wish to introduce another, complementary view of evaluation. I know of many formative evaluation tools that help students improve their ability to acquire knowledge or master a professional performance. And it is not my intention to analyze the state of the art in formative evaluation but to question the conclusions that are often taken for granted now in the practice of adult education. After all, data have no value unless one knows how to make sense of them.

Our picture of evaluation comes from the field of pedagogy. Testing and grading is an important theme in preparatory education for young people. The techniques of evaluation have passed through different stages. According to moods, contexts, and clienteles, these techniques have varied from traditional measurement to qualitative observation to self-assessment. Generally, the desire for scientific control and applicable generalizations has shifted now to an interest in local analysis. Recognizing the context of an educational program and the specific actors involved in it has a tendency to be seen as more important than the generalizability of results. The research done in this field of evaluation also has a tendency to abandon the rigor of quantitative treatment of data in favor of analysis of more qualitative sources of information. The summative function has also become less important than the formative function. The idea of control through evaluation is therefore less obvious for educators and not necessarily associated with the roles they have to play as evaluators. Evaluation is considered today more a support for regulations that might help a specific educational program attain its objectives than a scientific field of study leading to general rules.

Nevertheless, although the practice of evaluation has evolved, it remains an expression of power in the functioning of an organization. Education does not partake of the dynamics of only a class or group of adults. Any educational program takes place in a political or economic context and is partly an answer to a social demand. The objectives of education are not defined only by educators. Educators have an organizational status. They have to take their contracts seriously. They belong to a hierarchy. In some ways, evaluation is seen as a means for educators to bring truth to light. Pedagogy is still seen as instrumental, and its ends depend on the goals valued by an organization. Evaluation is typically one of the tools through which this instrumental function of pedagogy takes place. Although adult educators are working for an organization by which they are employed and paid, they have a tendency to try to escape this dependency and to forget how much their practice of evaluation unmasks the organizational connection.

It is not surprising that so many adult educators have been attracted by the idea of self-evaluation as it has been promoted by humanist psychology. In his book *Freedom to Learn*, Carl Rogers (1969) explained how the development of learning for an adult is closely related to the opportunity to evaluate its result. Educators do not like to recognize either their own power to evaluate or their dependency on the function of evaluation. They want to help their students learn in order to obtain a desired certificate or degree, but they like to think they are free to organize their jobs according to their own standards. They try to give to evaluation the meaning they attribute to learning. They might be open to the principle of controlling knowledge or behavior within the domain in which they teach, but they do not like the control of an external norm. In adult education so much has been said about the autonomy of the learner, it is difficult for educators to admit the contradiction between their approaches to evaluation and to learning.

Evaluation is an organizational requirement that has symbolic aspects and hidden motives. These may be seen from several points of view.

• There are economic reasons to evaluate a program, and they are clearly related to the budget invested. In private enterprise, continuing education is more and more analyzed in terms of return on investment. Even the learner often sees a program in terms of its immediate benefits.

• Evaluation has a political side that has to do with the function played by education in society. When innovation takes place in education, political authorities are expected to control its result. That explains why in Europe evaluation is bound up with any school reform. Evaluation produces data that are supposed to inform decision makers about the effects of organizational changes. In practice, evaluation adapts itself to the structure of an organization, and it can reinforce a hierarchy as well as facilitate change.

• Evaluation may also be justified by a social goal or personal system of values. In many societies it can be considered part of the culture. Used as the technology of teaching, it has been driven mainly by the goal of promoting democracy. The right to an education stands as a basic right in any society that proclaims itself a free society. The practice of evaluation has therefore served the purposes of school reform and worked against arbitrary selection. Benjamin Bloom (1954) developed his taxonomies in education with the idea that any learner could master the objectives of a program if his or her rhythm and way of learning were taken into serious consideration.

• Evaluation has a social dimension, and it becomes visible when schoolteachers or adult educators assist students who are about to be examined or who must pass any kind of test. Evaluation is frequently associated with the suffering that goes along with grades and diplomas. It requires encouragement and support. One of its functions is to facilitate guidance and counseling.

• Evaluation also carries psychological effects. As educational biographies demonstrate, we often tend to do our best in order to please another person. Students are proud to show their parents that they can succeed. Adults may feel guilty or ashamed around their employers or close family members if they fail. For learners, evaluation belongs partly to the world of the superego.

• Many adults remember how they were classified according to the grades they obtained in school. They have an image of themselves and their capacities that is related to comparisons between themselves and others. Evaluation goes with competition. It often becomes an event in which learners feel they must survive or succeed.

These different social demands that determine the practice of evaluation are not always seen by educators. Most of them consider themselves free to choose a practice of evaluation they believe is well adapted to the population with which they work. Yet evaluation as a pedagogical practice is always connected with a social organization. The responsibility of an adult educator in the domain of evaluation is clearly defined by the function he or she is supposed to play within the structure of an organization. The delusion of educators comes when they think they can escape traditional norms of evaluation for the sake of the goals they have for their student's learning. They forget how much the aims of education are imposed in any society or have to fit the structure of any organization. Evaluation reminds us that adult educators are asked to execute more than to conceive.

Displacing Evaluation to Another Object

My position is not to challenge the place of evaluation as an exercise of power or to refuse its function of control, but to introduce a dimension of research and reflection in the practice of evaluation. In opening such a dimension, defining the theoretical object of evaluation is the key task. To what kind of knowledge about adult education should it contribute? To what kind of theoretical questions does the practice of evaluation relate? Definition of the contribution of evaluation to theory is such a difficult task that educators often avoid it. Instead of clarifying the possible contribution of an evaluation in terms of objects on which the evaluation might focus, they satisfy themselves by centering on what they are asked to evaluate or, on the contrary, by setting their own aims and ignoring the norms they should respect. There is also sometimes a confusion of objects. Evaluating the students' performance may have the hidden objective of evaluating the teacher or the curriculum. The results obtained about students may then be used to evaluate the level of a curriculum or the productivity of a teacher.

The evaluation of products should be differentiated from the evaluation of actors. Evaluating students means something different from evaluating programs or organizations. If students fail, that failure could be their responsibility as well as the responsibility of their parents or of the school. Sometimes the responsibility is shared. Without a clear initial idea of what the evaluation should contribute, that is, without a clear purpose for the evaluation, any kind of data might be distorted and serve the purpose of any kind of objective. Many teachers agree to evaluate their teaching as long as it will help them to improve the methods they use. But they have the right to resist when the data collected ostensibly for this reason are then used to pass judgment on their way of teaching. The distrust teachers have for the practices of evaluation is often related to this lack of clarity about the intended object.

If students' products, educational programs, and educational systems are three distinctive objects of evaluation, we should also consider how objects might shift in the context of adult education. When participants in adult education are allowed to express their needs, the evaluation should reflect the meeting of those needs. But as any adult educator has experienced, the needs felt at the beginning of a program may radically evolve during the program. I remember working on an evaluation instrument addressed specifically to the objectives set by an adult educator for a parent education program. However, the group dynamics and the specific interests expressed by the parents required the educator to shift the program content, and the instrument I had prepared with him became useless. When adult education individualizes processes of learning, how does one perform a normative evaluation for a group or a class? When professionals are involved in a program to answer questions arising from their different daily activities, how can one control a common level of achievement?

My experience in adult education and the questions I had to face eventually convinced me to abandon the normative dimension of evaluation and to deal instead with processes and not products. It became clear to me that for the purpose of fostering adult learning, it was more important to know why and how adults learned than to prove that they had retained the content of a program or achieved its objectives. Evaluation is for me a source of information that identifies influences on the process of learning more than it names the results obtained. The norms of a program are a different object for evaluation from the dynamics of adults' learning processes. Adult learning became the object of evaluation for me when I realized that a clear idea about the product did not explain the reasons for learning, when I understood that the behavior of adult learners had to be analyzed more through the dynamics of a personal system than through measures of input and output. Moreover, this displacement of the object of evaluation led me to the biographical approach. The life history became the context in which adult learning, as a process, could be understood.

Thus, strangely enough, it was through the practice of evaluation that I understood that adults learn through a process whose dynamics result from the dynamics of their life histories. The limits of summative and even formative evaluations also convinced me that evaluation should not be limited to uses controlled by social scientists but should be opened up to participatory approaches. Educational evaluation is, generally speaking, confined to setting criteria for diplomas or for showing program successes and does not analyze the way educational programs regulate the process of learning. In adult education, research serves the market of continuing education more than it provides a better understanding of adults' ways of learning. Years before I began working with educational biographies, I realized how necessary it is to evaluate adults with a participative methodology and to associate them with a research project. They are more able than any other researcher to identify their own reactions, the difficulties they have experienced, and what they really learned through an educational program. When the dynamics of learning become the theme of a dialogue among students and between students and their teacher, evaluation takes on a new meaning. Qualitative research done with the participants themselves is certainly not easy. Students are surprised by it and sometimes distrustful.

Seeing Evaluation as Interpretation

As the research I discuss in this chapter shows, I have explored with some of my own students this participative and qualitative methodology. After these various explorations in the field of evaluation I came to the conclusion that evaluation in adult education should be mainly an interpretation based on data coming from educational activities. With whatever methodology the data are gathered, without interpretation they are meaningless. The scientific approach depended for years on the idea of an objective reality that could be grasped by empirico-analytical metrics. Employing an evaluation based on a quasi-experimental design made me question this assumption. It made me aware that adult learning was closely related to the perspective of life history (Dominicé, 1979). As I have said, evaluation was for me the key that opened the door to the world of the biographical approach, and in my practice of educational biography interpretation remains a priority. The seminar participants and I interpret a narrative that is already an interpretation by one learner of his or her educational life history. The work of research becomes a work of interpretation that questions the language used and its references as well as deepens the understanding of reality. Evaluation as research produces a better and more subtle interpretation of what really happens in education.

In a program organized as continuing education for adult educators by the university, I used the opportunity of the evaluation to suggest an exercise of interpretation. I asked the participants at the end of the program to fill out three columns on a sheet of paper, one in which they named the activities, such as lectures, group discussions, and required papers, they considered sources of learning; one in which they described the specific content coming out of each source of learning; and one in which they identified the form or process of the learning itself. I knew they would be selective, and they were. Some lectures and reading assignments were not even mentioned. Self-directed learning had an important place. One participant's first source of learning, for example, was working on his papers. Some sources of learning mentioned were not formal parts of the program, such as learning from other participants' vocational experience. I made it clear to the participants that I was not evaluating the program but the processes through which they considered they had learned something. I was not expecting value judgments, but reflections about adult learning. I was not looking for negative criticism of teachers or lecturers. I thought it was important for the learners, again all adult educators, to identify the loci and the forms of learning that might come out of a curriculum. This type of evaluation could easily lead to more systematic research.

Educators are always trying to improve program planning. They want to master educational objectives, and they like to make teaching efficient. However, I believe it is an illusion to think that evaluation can lead one to conceive the right or the best program. Education cannot escape the individual process through which learning finally becomes meaningful. For me, the shaping of learning is the most useful object of evaluation. It is indeed important to discover what turned out to be meaningful for a learner, but such a research theme has no guaranteed conclusion. Learning will always be what learners do with education. The reasons learning happens will always reveal something that surprises us, and that should encourage educators to remain modest.

Summary

This chapter is an attempt to expand the boundaries of educational biography. Training can become an approach to research, and research can be part of the training program. My own experiences have shown both the advantages and the difficulties of such a perspective.

Evaluation opened the door of the biographical approach for me. It made me relate adult learning with life history. Life history is a context in which learning can be analyzed as a process and often as a response to the process of growing up.

The first experiment I discuss, conducted in the context of training adult educators working as directors of continuing education programs in various firms and multinational corporations, used evaluation to help the trainees put words to what they considered they had learned during the program.

The second case shows what kind of itinerary adult students follow as they fulfill the requirements of a program. Adult learners have studying tactics that teachers very often ignore. As they structure their own curricula, they are influenced by both the professional and the personal aspects of their life histories. They have a tendency to take into consideration what they already know as they consider how to deal with material they have previously ignored or that they feel is foreign to them.

What was actually my first approach, although I discuss it third in this chapter, invited students to prepare a kind of diary in which they commented on what happened in the class, sometimes expressing surprise over the content of the course itself and my personal teaching methodology and how they adapted to it. Often they compared these teaching methods with previous teaching methods. They seemed to see their adult education as part of a process that started during their school years and so it was affected by learning experiences during that early schooling.

Evaluation is an opportunity to reflect on what happens in a class or a program in term of learning processes. This understanding of evaluation contrasts with the current primary function of evaluation, which is to exercise power. This dimension of control is therefore analyzed in its different facets.

Learning is not an object of research for most evaluation. When we take adult learning as the object of evaluation, we engage in a methodological displacement. Educational biography as a training and research approach could assist in this displacement, inspiring a primarily instrumental practice of evaluation.

One of the tasks of evaluation is interpretation of data. The main task in using educational biography is to work on the interpretation presented by an adult learner. The process a group goes through in understanding more about adult learning through the life histories of its members is also a process of interpreting data. Thus evaluation and educational biography might contribute to the same theoretical purpose.

Chapter Nine

Creating Conditions for Successful Learning in Adult Life

This final chapter summarizes the general purpose of this book and the main themes I have developed. It was the practice of evaluation that convinced me that adults' learning has to be analyzed within the context of individuals' life histories. Educational biography has become the methodology I use to identify how adults learn through the meaningful experiences of their life history. I first used the biographical approach at the university with my own students, who happened to be mostly in their thirties. Most of what I do today in applying the life history approach to adult education comes from this first experiment.

Educational Biography and Adult Learning

I described in Chapter Two how my students prepare educational biography narratives in oral and written versions in small groups and how these narratives are interpreted within the groups. In a final phase, they analyze the main themes coming out of the discussion about the narratives. The questions members of the group raise at the beginning about life history taken as a learning process remain the theoretical object of each biographical approach.

Educational biography is not an autobiography nor is it a full life history. It is a version of a life history that an adult is invited to construct in order to think about the dynamics of his or her learning. As discussion proceeds in the small groups, the students experience what I call an *echo effect,* as the interpretations of the learning experiences in one narrative challenge the interpretations of the others. In this process, most of the students realize the key role of interpretation in their learning process.

I have also mentioned the length of time that an educational biography approach might take. Longer times seem preferable. My seminar takes two semesters, for example, although, as I described, the University of Geneva does offer a more concentrated schedule for adult educators and other professionals who cannot attend the regular university class. For the last three years we have explored a shorter approach in the context of various training programs for adult educators; however, this is intended to sensitize adult educators to the power of life experiences as they affect ways of learning rather than to offer them real training in the method.

Educational biography may be used in various ways in training programs for adult educators, as is already the case at the University of Geneva in Switzerland and at Columbia University in New York. Each application must of course be appropriate to the specific social environment. Moreover, as I have also been describing, adults' reflection on their life experiences offers an opportunity to explore new paths of research, including participatory research. Participants become partners, and research itself becomes an educational process that helps these partners discover how research can become part of a transformative learning process.

Throughout this book I have tried to show the benefits of biographical research for adult educators and learners. In publishing this book I want to invite the reader to a dialogue. The importance of understanding the ways adults learn encouraged me to take the time to write this book in a language that is not my own. We all tend to maintain our educational practices in the tradition of our local cultures, yet today we live in an international world. The intention of this book is intercultural. By presenting to North American practitioners of adult education research that has its origin in the French-speaking part of Europe, I wish to invite these practitioners to discover how they can use this approach on their own terms. At each of the meetings of the European Society for Research in the Education of Adults (ESREA), the attendees have realized the great extent to which life history concepts and methodologies applied to adult education result in educational biography approaches that are dependent upon local cultural contexts. German, Polish, British, and French, each group of educators recognized a different intellectual tradition. This diversity of application should offer adult educators and researchers who would like to enlarge upon their own experiences a context for reflection. Indeed, offering an understanding of the vital role of cultural dynamics is one of the primary goals of this book.

Learning is very personal, but it is a collective process as well. Learning takes place in the global context of an adult life; therefore there is no formal learning without a constant interaction with the social environment. Family, friends, and colleagues are part of our learning experiences. Learning is basically a process of identification with both social and cultural sources. It is also a process of becoming more autonomous, a process through which adults have to find the right distance from the cultural norms that shaped their education. Learning to be oneself, whatever else one has to learn in life, is the main trend of each life history.

Dialogue with Adult Educators

It has never been easy to combine theory and practice in education. Practitioners often challenge researchers about the relevance of their theoretical contribution. This is especially true when educators feel that they are building their competency primarily from their own professional experience.

In this concluding chapter I want to address myself more directly to such practitioners and take their skepticism as a challenge, and therefore in the following sections I suggest some issues that might guide an open dialogue with educators working with adults.

Models cannot guarantee success. Pedagogy and andragogy should remain at the level of means or tools. Any principle for action has to be put in a specific context to be understood. To some well-known authors, such as Malcolm Knowles (1973), andragogy appears a more appropriate term and concept than pedagogy to describe teaching the clientele of adult education. Whatever term we use to name our work, we have to specify the sociological and psychological characteristics of the adults we have in mind and analyze each situation in its full complexity. Planning and selecting instruments remain useful for organizing a curriculum, the content of teaching, but both educators and learners will always provide elements of surprise and variation in any program.

Scientific data and methodologies may be helpful for formalizing or generalizing an educational program or experience, but the knowledge of education that I call clinical knowledge is produced only through a dialogue between actors such as teachers and learners. The guidelines I am proposing have to be seen in this light. They are hypotheses on which action may be based, and they should be understood as such. If I stress the idea of a dialogue, it is because I have found pedagogy and andragogy to take their shape out of this unending debate between actors. As actors, educators have had different experiences, varying capacities for analyzing and interpreting what they are doing, and even different goals and values. Thus they cannot be molded into a single type of educator who takes a single set approach. Moreover, despite their various approaches practitioners are seldom wrong in a chosen approach as long as they try to be explicit about what they are doing and are able to share its meaning with their students.

Therefore one of my goals is to empower educators to become more reflective. In my classes I have always refused to teach adult educators what to do. I like first to establish a style of communication with the practitioners that allows us to share our experiences, hopes, and tactics. However, this mutual reflection requires practitioners to have the discipline to observe the situation in which they work and to take the time to write about it. Preparing educational biographies provides the conditions for this mutual reflection and interpretation.

Educational Biography Enhances Learners' Capacity

Learning results from interaction between learners and environments. This statement reflects Piaget's theories of intellectual development. The same idea occurs in adults' oral and written narratives as adults address the topic of their own education. It also fits my understanding from my own experience with students. Adults may be able to adapt to a situation, complete a program, or pass an examination, but the meaning of a program is not shown by these events but by their personal involvement as learners. As several examples in previous chapters have shown, learning belongs to the process of finding one's identity as an adult. Looking at their life history as a whole helps adult learners realize what characterizes their relation to knowledge, that is, how they construct their own knowledge. One woman, for example, writes in her narrative: "To provoke my father's sensitiveness when he was concerned about topics which made both my parents irritated has been the motor in the development of some of my knowledge." They become aware, for example, how much their patterns of schooling and studying depend on their parents' expectations. Many women were not supposed to study at the university, and when they finally decided later in their lives to join a university program, they had to fight against the relation to knowledge they had experienced and absorbed earlier in their journeys. Another example of the relation to knowledge is the difficulty many adults have in trusting experience as a worthwhile source of reflection and learning. That they have this difficulty is clear from their biographical narratives. Yet adults remember and use the knowledge they feel they have gained by themselves. It does not mean they see themselves as self-educated, but they consider they have learned something when they have, in one way or another, been personally committed and active in the process of gaining knowledge.

Adult educators should know that adults vary in their ways of learning. Educators cannot therefore master all their students' ways of learning when they teach or work with a group. They must keep in mind that whatever they do as educators and regardless of the quality of their pedagogical contribution, each adult has his or her own approach to learning. Adult educators might feel useless or inappropriate confronting this diversity. They might feel discouraged when they witness the results of their teaching. It is always painful for educators to realize that the content of learning belongs to the learner. As they prepare their own educational biographies, many adult educators are surprised to discover how much this has been true in their own lives.

Learning how to learn and learning to be autonomous in the learning process are considered more and more to be the priorities in the continuing education of adults. How can we help adults discover their own way of learning? The biographical approach might be one of the answers to educating adults to be in charge of their own ways of learning.

In today's society, adults are often considered the clients of educational products. Their way to learn is more and more prepared for them in the form of ready-made kits. Most jobs demand a capacity to learn. In order to remain competitive, adults should be able to find the right information, use available resources, and be creative with whatever learning means are provided. Sources of knowledge today are multiple. Taking seminars and workshops is not enough. Longer schooling and more intensive continuing education leading to technical qualifications have gained more importance than high levels of cultural heritage. A sensitivity to their own biographies and ways of learning might be a counterpart that would help adults be autonomous and creative in their use of adult and continuing education.

Competence in today's world demands personal and social qualifications. Being educated for a specific job is no longer adequate for economic survival. In every sector of life, adults are having to gain learning skills in order to face changes and adapt to new challenges. They have to work on their personal development in this always changing cultural environment. They have to improve their basic health through a healthier life style. They have to deal with social issues, such as urban violence, reductions in mandated social supports, and modifications in their daily lives. They have to understand actions by their governments even when they do not agree with the decisions made. The educational biography approach has helped many adult educators discover the value of experiential social learning, including what adults have learned through the challenges of their lives.

Today, due to the general turbulence of our societies, there is a reawakening to the value of a perspective of *lifelong learning* (Bélanger, 1992). Adults have not only to fight to keep their jobs in weak economic conditions or to find new ones if they do become jobless but also to face the inadequacy of most answers given by traditional organizations such as churches or political parties. They have to renew their personal value systems in the midst of a vacuum of beliefs. During the 1960s, international organizations developed the notion of lifelong learning as a kind of chronological and ecological understanding of education. The subsequent economic crisis had a tendency to reduce adult education to programs of continuing professional education. It has therefore become difficult for most adult educators to talk about education beyond the boundaries of job qualifications. Using an educational biography approach might be a good stepping-stone for them, enlarging their view of education so they can concretely understand how adult life itself provides a global context for learning. Adult educators are to a certain extent double agents. They have to meet the requirements of their job to teach certain content and they have to allow space for the dreams of the adults with whom they are working. How can they be open to the latter need if they do not remain aware of the dreams of their own unlived lives?

As Many Life Histories as Adults

Any educator has to find a balance between the principles derived from his or her past experiences and the surprises occurring in each new situation. Groups of learners always have both similarities and differences. As parents, what we learn with our first child we can apply to the second. However, we also have to be ready to discover with each new child something we did not know with the others. Similarly, even though the general characteristics of adult life are recognizable in every adult, each adult also has his or her own life history. For educators, knowledge is always contextual. This is why I speak in this book about educators' clinical knowledge.

The life history approach offers a theoretical frame of reference that helps adult educators understand how each individual can contribute to the understanding of a larger population. School failure, for instance, is a fundamental life experience that influences an adult's vocational choice, but finding the exact meaning given to this experience of failure by a person requires listening to that single person. French sociologist Vincent de Gaulejac has studied what he calls the "family novel." Each family builds its novel out of its own heritage and out of sociological trends, and each adult builds his or her own life within a family structure. As Gaulejac (1987) says: "Adult identity is torn between permanence and contrast, between similarity and singularity, between reproduction and differentiation, between the past as background and openness to the future in the present" (p. 98).

Yet awareness of their own uniqueness is often lacking among adult learners. Instead of comparing adult students to a norm, educators should try to empower them as individual learners. Again, this is for me a main task of adult education. Adults are frequently afraid of the changes that learning implies. They resist a deeper understanding of their own dynamics. They have doubts about the new attitudes or behavior expected of them as the result of a workshop. Helping adults to be confident about their capacities to learn has to be considered a starting point. Adult educators have a wide responsibility in this domain. Biographical narratives, by giving students access to the dynamics between their own lives and learning, open the way to a better understanding of the conditions for learning in adult life. In my experience of using educational biography, I have always gained new pictures of the students after hearing their narratives. Their reasons for studying so late in life at the university become obvious. I know what they trust in themselves and what they feel it important to improve upon or to overcome. Out of the typical anonymous academic context, where students are defined through superficial observations, they suddenly appeared in the richness of their individual persons.

There is a psychology of adult education that is more helpful for adult educators than the psychology of adulthood (Mader, 1992, pp. 142–154). Adults' narratives tell us that adults have an image of themselves based on the grades and diplomas they have gained during their school life. Working on their life histories might help them discover some meaningful learning experiences that can reduce the weight of the bad memories they have of painful school learning experiences.

The phase of interpretation might be the occasion for a meeting of teacher and students to discuss key questions regarding adult learning. Questions involving students' images of themselves as learners, their artistic commitment compared to their intellectual study, and the personal and social implications of university studies for their partners and children are mostly unexamined in the academic scene. According to my students' reports, the practice of educational biography has often helped them understand their own dynamics.

Oneself and Others

Most adults have an image of themselves as learners that results from family members' and teachers' opinions. Evaluation therefore plays a key role in the dynamics of learning as adult student go back to school. "My school grades were demonstrating, year after year, the socioemotional impact of my teachers," wrote an adult student in her narrative. Adult students remain dependent on judgments given by others. They expect evaluation to provide evidence from somebody else that they have learned something. Adults also learn in order to please others such as parents, spouses, friends, or teachers. In their formal education, adults receive support from the guidance, teaching, or coaching given to them by educators in various roles. Preparing educational biographies helps adults understand these interpersonal influences in their lives.

Adult biographical narratives are full of references to the people who played an important role in the individuals' learning processes. Insofar as learning is primarily considered a way to assert oneself, it is mostly a social experience. Experiential learning is related mostly to encounters, partnerships, and other meaningful relationships, although it is also sometimes associated with a time of being alone. Parents, brothers and sisters, friends, lovers, partners, and employers are mentioned. We have all learned from the joy and pain shared with or caused by others. The educator is consequently only one of many companions in a life history. For educators this partnership is even more difficult because they sometimes have to pay for the poor performance of former teachers. Adult students project onto their teachers expectations and attitudes that have little to do with the educators themselves. Any educator knows how adult students can be critical for reasons that have nothing to do with the current educational situation. For example, I have become aware from the narratives and comments made during group discussions how much women's relation to academic knowledge is influenced by women's relationships with their fathers. I have also became aware that I was sometimes a father figure for women who expressed ambivalence toward studying at the university. They projected onto me their father's expectation as well as their father's social rejection of university studies.

Personal development is widely associated with social relationships. Thus group dynamics have an important place in adult education, and many adult workshops are primarily oriented toward human communication. Throughout their lives, adults keep working on their social relationships. When an adult quotes others in his or her narrative, it is often because these individuals have led the author to new discoveries about himself or herself or about communication and social relations. In both formal and informal learning contexts a great amount of time is spent on regulating processes, reaching agreement, and contracting with others. When learners mention the benefits of their studies at university, I am always impressed by the place they give to the personal relationships they have had with their professors. Evaluation procedures are also a source of discussion, bargaining, and sometimes conflicts. The resolution of conflicts and the making of new agreements concerning daily life among families and couples are often considered learning experiences. Possibly one of the basic lessons that must be learned in adult life is how to remain oneself and at the same time live with others. The struggle for this balance is one of the most prominent features in many educational biographies I have read. Often, learning experiences and educational activities are devoted to this complex existential learning.

Cultural Diversity in the Learning Process

Throughout this book I have tried to avoid overgeneralization and to remain aware of important diversities. For instance, women and men differ in their reactions to knowledge (Gilligan, 1982). The biographical narratives I have read and heard illustrate that men are more inclined to separate professional from personal lives or emotion from reasoning, whereas women are more globally present in any situation. As many surveys have shown, for men advancement in working life is the main impetus for obtaining adult education, whereas women have broader expectations for their learning. This cultural difference tends to be taken more seriously in recent literature. However, adult learners are still more frequently classified according to school background, age, or professional experience than according to sociocultural diversity or gender. Yet the narratives often underline gender distinctions. Women, for example, as we saw earlier, call up various roles when they describe themselves as learners; they are "woman, spouse, mother, and professional." For women, learning more often finds its meaning outside their professional itinerary.

Adults have internalized cultural models. These models reflect images, expectations, and wishes deriving from their genealogical family's cultural roots. Parents, other family members, and sometimes people in the local community project their own expectations. "In my family as well as the family of my social environment," said one student, "when the first child was a man there was a hope that he would become a priest." This statement does not come from the nineteenth century. In addition, fathers still expect their sons to take over their businesses. Mothers still hope their daughters will accomplish what they have not been able or allowed to realize.

Educational biographies could be analyzed from an anthropological perspective and contribute to the field of the anthropology of education. The narratives emphasize the unavoidable place of culture in the education of adults. By listening to and reading educational biographies, I have learned some cultural characteristics of the different regions of my own, small country that act as foundations in the learning process. For instance, the political choice made by a grandfather, the time spent in a religious high school, the respect for the weather in a farming environment are deep cultural references that never disappear and will always nourish the interpretation of life events. It is again important to be aware of the enduring influence of these cultural backgrounds in a society in which the popular concept of culture tends to be reduced to the patterns within a local organization or industrial firm.

Individuals' value systems have a land of origin. Money, for instance, has different values according to family backgrounds. It might be a key factor in a choice made to continue one's education or it might have no influence at all. Needs and also dreams have cultural and social origins. For many adults the need to improve their status or to make more money is often more important in their choice to join a program of continuing education than is the desire to learn. This is particularly true in a society in which the competition for jobs makes continuing education an obligation and thus just another level of schooling for most adults. Making adult education important and available for areas of life other than employment is a new challenge for adult educators. In this world dominated by the unidimensional cultural models imposed by media and publicity, we have a tendency to overlook the reality of cultural differences.

However, even if adult education has become a market, the learning process will always remain individual. Of course by individual I do not mean emotional or private. The individual learning process does not belong, as some authors suggest, to the world of the inner self. There is a rationality, or logic, of the subjective, and the distance we see between objective and subjective has to be reduced, according to French sociologist Alain Touraine (1992) in his brilliant book *Critique de la modernité* (Critique of modernity). Education needs to be both an individual and a collective process. Learning has to be considered the process of a social actor involved as the subject of his or her life. Biographical narratives are testimonies of a life history that is always, as Ferrarotti (1983) has said, a "singular universe."

Continuing and Discontinuing Education

Economics have become the predominant force in our society. As a result, continuing education is taking the place of adult education. Continuing education is an investment in the field of industrial production, whereas, earlier in this century, adult education was primarily associated with popular education. The movement of emancipation that characterized literacy campaigns (Freire, 1970), popular education among the workers unions, and better access to vocational adult education has turned with the development of continuing education into a kind of compulsory schooling for adults. If they want to keep their jobs or pursue a new career ambition, adults have to continue their education.

However, if we are to maintain learning as a priority of adult education, a broader perspective is needed. Aspects of the popular education heritage, such as voluntary learning activities, should be preserved, and the lifelong learning perspective should be reinterpreted, as it has been in the context of the European Community.

The idea of *discontinuous education* was created some years ago during a short and informal meeting of American, French, and Swiss researchers in adult education, organized by Jack Mezirow and myself in New York. The concept offers a counterperspective, a kind of polemical rationale for adult education seen from the point of view of educational biographies. It is an attempt to break away from the organizational logic of an education that simply is *continuing* what has been started earlier in school. In today's world, life can no longer be seen in terms of a career. Job insecurity obliges most adults to face and make meaningful the discontinuity of their lives.

The biographical approach opens the programmed world of education to the unknown, personal world of discontinuity. Adult students have their own rhythms. Learning occurs in a variety of styles that operate within individuals' personal systems. As I mentioned earlier in this book, according to one participant who analyzed the biographies of a group, "we all build ourselves around a key problem we are trying to solve all our life." The form each person gives to his or her life has to meet with the discontinuity or the incoherence of the solutions he or she find. Learning goes back and forth. The life stages we follow are never logical. We remain rebellious against ourselves even when we accept who we are. For instance, as adults people keep relating to the adolescence they had or did not have. This sort of discontinuity has to be recognized by educators who should focus on learners and not only on programs. Adults change, even as they conform to a formal setting. Their motives and their ways of learning unfold according to an internal logic. Their style of learning has to be explained within the larger context of their life history.

Adult Learning in a Changing World

Adults have to adapt to a world that is very different from the world of their formal education. The narratives make obvious what people have learned beyond their formal education. Spending a year abroad in their teenage years or later for their work and traveling on a limited budget and without too much planning in a totally different economic or social context are experiences of social learning that are often mentioned. Whenever people have to find a new job and adapt to a new working environment, they enter a process of social learning. In today's world, high technology requires many workers and employees to undergo such a process. According to the narratives, more tragic circumstances, such as losing a relative or being a refugee, are also sources of deep learning.

Adults do not seem to learn what they know socially and politically from being in a class or by watching television. Their frame of reference comes from what they have experienced and practiced in associations, social groups, and political movements. What I have understood through the biographies about social learning is clear. Adults build their frames of reference on the basis of their social or political experiences and commitments. Many adults who grew up during the sixties and the seventies mention that political involvement has played an important role in their education. They learned part of what they know as citizens when they had to fight in a group against higher rent rates, when they were part of a peace movement, or when they were working within the structures of political groups or parties. These fronts and causes have been partly deserted. But what I heard through the narratives has convinced me that social and political learning comes out of social and political action, even if today most people think they are learning from watching television or reading the paper when they are in fact only following the news.

Our democracies have partly lost the kind of social learning that is present in the narratives of adults over thirty. Political commitment has become a task for politicians only. Associations are clamoring for leadership, and voluntary organizations are complaining about lack of membership. Social experiences occur more often within small ethnic groups. The sense of being active in society is much less a source of learning. The social learning introduced by industrial management does not go beyond behavior within the company. In most countries a reduction of state budgets or an increase in public taxes is not a matter of reflection. People fight for their own budget and do not analyze the economic crisis in the collective context of their society. Why would they change their minds unless they had an opportunity to commit themselves to concrete political action? Politicians have learned to simplify the sociopolitical scene in order to justify simple solutions. Instead of contributing to the political education of adults, of the citizens of a democratic society, they attempt merely to influence public opinion toward their policies. We live, however, in a rapidly changing society in which we ceaselessly have to socially adapt. The world of politics seems to offer fewer and fewer opportunities for social learning. Because biographical narratives will remain, whatever the world situation, a method of diagnosing how adults have learned what they know, these narratives will always give adult educators an opportunity to grasp the cultural world of adults. Educational biographies will always give educators access to the evolving context of adult socialization.

We have reached such a level of crisis in Western society that I believe if older adults do not offer, on the basis of what they have learned in their lives, ways to discover a more global frame of reference, the younger generations will lock themselves in their private worlds. The question of the projects to which younger people can commit themselves today becomes an important cultural issue. This issue is central for adult education and should be a matter of deep concern for all professionals who call themselves adult educators. Perhaps the time has come to reinforce an intergenerational dialogue in which an exchange of educational biographies could take place, as has sometimes happened in my classes between students of two different generations.

Another changing area of learning is health care. Patient education has become important in the field of medicine. People with chronic disease are being asked to take better care of their health by learning about their disease in order to have a better quality of life or simply to survive. This is true for diabetics and asthmatics, for example, and the problem is similar in other fields. Unless people take care of their environment, unless they build new democratic objectives for societies, they will slowly destroy their quality of life. Many resolutions are taken by governments and by international organizations. The statements are clear and the problems well analyzed, but the solutions, in terms of educating citizens and mobilizing new community actions, are poor and very abstract. If we do not find ways to educate people in their role as citizens of this world, there is no hope for the survival of the environment and the inhabitants of the planet. Biographical approaches could give a better view of the processes through which adults change and learn to act differently. Educational biography is a tool that could help societies found political resolutions on the real dynamics of adult social learning. For example, those of us who are the European members of the International Association for Life History Applied to Adult Education network on life history and biographical methodology performed as a first experiment a biographical approach to our forthcoming European Community citizenship. We shared oral narratives in small groups, and in our analyses one of things we realized was how strong our images coming out of our personal experiences of World War II remained.

On Being an Adult Educator

Adult educators have their own life histories and should not forget to work on interpreting those histories. Being an educator of adults should not be narrowly defined as a professional status within an organization. As I have discovered through a research project, the people of the first, pioneering generation of adult educators (Knowles, 1984) are now beginning to retire. Because these pioneers had the opportunity to design their jobs and brought with them knowledge from a variety of backgrounds, such as engineering, psychology, and social work, the present contract conditions for adult educators are better. As we continue to develop this profession today, we should not forget this creative heritage even if we have to redefine the profession of adult educator in light of the new economic challenges.

Because the interpersonal dimension of teaching and learning is often neglected in training adult educators, one benefit of asking educators to prepare educational biographies is that they may realize to what extent schooling is a socialization process influenced by teachers, as I have shown throughout this book. Their profession is a profession in which human relationships play a key role. It is not because they feel mature or are adults themselves that they are able to teach other adults.

If adult educators have an opportunity to work on their own life histories and their own formal and informal learning experiences, they will be more aware of the factors present in the process of adult learning. We do know that adult educators who have worked on their personal development come to realize how important it is for them to be open to their own dynamics in their reactions to others. Teaching centered on the learner does not mean much for educators who are centered on the content. Unless they have an opportunity to analyze an example of their own experiential learning, they will not understand the meaning of being centered on the learner. Unless they can understand the dialectic between formal and informal learning, they will not relate the content of what they teach to the more global life of their students. The opportunity to prepare an educational biography has to be offered in the training programs of adult educators. It will open new horizons for the understanding of their own continuing education. It will allow groups of educators to share the problems they meet in their profession and to see them in a new light.

As Huberman (1990) has explained, there are several stages in the life cycle of teachers. They experience both enjoyment of and self-doubt about their status. They have good feelings as well as bad impressions about themselves as educators. Enthusiasm, creativity, retreat, and routine are examples of chronological stages that are personal as well as social. A biographical approach that would help adult educators be more explicit about the stages of their own professional life histories might provide a context in which they could set the objectives of their own continuing education.

Adult educators are no longer working only in more or less academic classes or study groups. In a changing world, more so than their colleagues working only in schools, they have an opportunity to evolve the image of their profession. They might organize adult and continuing education in the context of a company. They might work closely with human resource managers or offer specialized learning in a scientific or a technical field. Instead of devoting their entire career to teaching, adult educators might work in continuing or adult education for some years as just one stage of their professional lives. In the present context of our societies, there is, as I described, a close interaction between employment and continuing education. Adult educators have to be open to the new task of consulting and offering instruction within the human resource department. By being sensitive to biographical transformations in their own professional lives, adult educators will gain a better perspective, one that allows them to be better judges of the changes in the life story of their profession. Many educators today have a tendency to buy the latest successful product in educational technology offered on the market. It is also true that a simple version of the life history approach will soon be offered on the market; it may be available as you read this. However, if adult educators are well informed about the use of educational biography, they can preserve the necessary deeper meaning in the life history approach.

In the present economic context, adult educators have to change the frame of reference in which they think about themselves as professionals. Education is now seen as a link in the chain of production. It has become a tool for the world of high technology. Biographical approaches such as educational biography might contribute to once again emphasizing the personal side of learning as well as enlarging the idea of education so it has a more global perspective (as I have seen many adult educators do). As they come to realize how social experiences influence adult learning processes, adult educators should develop a more systemic view and move between different levels of reality. Some things we know from personal relationships or personal life events. Some things we learn by finding our way through social and political events. Today, economy and finance dominate our theoretical references. Adult educators should know how to deal with the truth as well as the myths of economic realities, because the economic scene determines the future of adult education as well as defining the status and the new frontiers of adult educators.

Learning, as the biographical approach allows us to understand it, requires the courage to change. As a researcher in the field of adult education, I feel the urgency of contributing to a theory of learning that is close to a theory of life changes. As adult educators we have to be able to contribute to the production of new knowledge. This production of new knowledge about adult learning and change is not only the task of university adult educators but the work of all adult educators in other contexts as well. I have introduced the idea of clinical knowledge for the field of education. By their involvement as practitioners and on the basis of their experiences and observations, all adult educators could contribute to research. They need to be recognized as potential researchers by university researchers, who can give them the recognition and the means to contribute to this new knowledge. I am convinced that the practice of adult education, as it is taking place in most universities around the world, has opened a new era for the future of the universities as well as for the future of adult education. Scholars do not take enough advantage of the wealth of experience and knowledge gained by adult education practitioners. This wide experience has to be formalized in domains in which scientific knowledge is inadequate to educate adults.

Participatory and formative research in these domains would give universities a chance to renew the epistemological foundations of the human and social sciences. Challenging social problems such as reducing drug abuse, coping with the complex pathologies of long-term diseases, and stemming the rise of unemployment among younger and older adults are clamoring for effective action that this research might address. It would give many organizations a larger understanding of education based on the very nature of adult learning. By being active in this new adventure, adult educators will certainly create new conditions for successful learning in adult life.

References

Alheit, P. "The Biographical Approach to Adult Education." In W. Mader (ed.), *Adult Education in the Federal Republic of Germany: Scholarly Approaches and Professional Practice*. Vancouver: University of British Columbia, 1992.

Alheit, P. *Taking the Knocks: Youth Unemployment and Biography: A Qualitative Analysis*. London: Cassell, 1994.

Alheit, P. "Biographical Learning: Theoretical Outline, Challenges and Contradictions of a New Approach in Adult Education." In P. Alheit, A. Bron-Wojciechowska, E. Brugger, and P. Dominicé (eds.), *The Biographical Approach in European Adult Education*. Vienna: Verband Wiener Volksbildung, 1995.

Bélanger, P. "L'éducation des adultes et le vieillissement des populations: Tendances et enjeux" (Adult education facing the aging process). *International Review of Education*, 1992, 38(4), 343–362.

Belkaïd, M. *Normaliennes en Algérie* (School teacher trainees in Algeria). Paris: Editions L'Harmattan, 1998.

Bertaux, D. "L'approche biographique: Sa validité méthodologique, ses potentialités" (The biographical approach: Methodological validity and potential). *Cahiers Internationaux de Sociologie*, 1980 (special issue), pp. 197–225.

Birren, J. E., and Deutchman, D. E. (eds.). *Guiding Autobiography Groups for Older Adults: Exploring the Fabric of Life*. Baltimore, Md.: Johns Hopkins University Press, 1991.

Bloom, B. S. (ed.). *Taxonomy of Educational Objectives*. White Plains, N.Y.: Longman, 1954.

Bogdan, R. C., and Biklen, S. K. *Qualitative Research for Education: An Introduction to Theory and Method*. Needham Heights, Mass.: Allyn & Bacon, 1982.

Boutinet, J. P. *Psychologie de la vie adulte* (The psychology of adult life). Paris: Presses Universitaires de France, 1995.

Bron-Wojciechowska, A. "The Use of Life History Approach in Adult Education Research." In P. Alheit, A. Bron-Wojciechowska, E. Brugger, and

P. Dominicé (eds.), *The Biographical Approach in European Adult Education*. Vienna: Verband Wiener Volksbildung, 1995.

Brookfield, S. *Understanding and Facilitating Adult Learning*. San Francisco: Jossey-Bass, 1986.

Brookfield, S. *Developing Critical Thinkers: Challenging Adults to Explore Alternative Ways of Thinking and Acting*. San Francisco: Jossey-Bass, 1987.

Brugger, E. "Biographical Learning Resources in Life-Stories: Illiterates." In P. Alheit, A. Bron-Wojciechowska, E. Brugger, and P. Dominicé (eds.), *The Biographical Approach in European Adult Education*. Vienna: Verband Wiener Volksbildung, 1995.

Cahiers Internationaux de Sociologie, 1980 (special issue).

Candy, P. C. *Self-Direction for Lifelong Learning*. San Francisco: Jossey-Bass, 1991.

Casey, L. *I Answer with My Life: Life Histories of Women Teachers Working for Social Change*. New York: Routledge, 1994.

Catani, M. *Journal de Mohammed: Un Algérien en France parmi 800,000 autres* (The life of Mohammed: An Algerian in France among 800,000 others). Paris: Stock, 1973.

Catani, M. "Susciter une histoire de vie sociale est d'abord affaire de relation" (Creating a social life history is primarily a matter of relationship). Paper presented at the World Congress of Sociology, Upsala, 1978.

Catani, M., and Mazé, S. *Tante Suzanne: Une histoire de vie sociale* (Aunt Suzanne: A social life history). Paris: Méridiens Klincksieck, 1982.

Cranton, P. *Understanding and Promoting Transformative Learning: A Guide for Educators of Adults*. San Francisco: Jossey-Bass, 1995.

Cross, K. P. *Adults as Learners: Increasing Participation and Facilitating Learning*. San Francisco: Jossey-Bass, 1981.

Daloz, L. *Effective Teaching and Mentoring*. San Francisco: Jossey-Bass, 1986.

Daussien, B. *Biographie und Geschlecht: Zur biographischen Konstruction sozialer Wirklichkeit in Frauenlebensgeschichten* (Biography and gender: About the biographical construction of reality in women's life history). Bremen: Im Druck Donat Verlag, 1995.

de Certeau, M. "Le roman psychoanalytique et son institution: Les contraintes institutionnelles, rencontre franco-latino-américaine" (The psychoanalytical novel and its institution: The institutional constraints [French-Latino-American Conference]). Unpublished manuscript, Paris, 1981.

de Villers, G. *L'histoire de vie comme méthode clinique* (Life history as a clinical approach). Cahiers de la Section des Sciences de l'Education, no. 72. Geneva: Université de Genève, 1993.

Demazière, D., and Dubar, C. *Analyser les entretiens biographiques* (Analyzing biographical interviews). Paris: Editions Nathan, 1997.

Denzin, N. *Interpretive Biography*. Thousand Oaks, Calif.: Sage, 1989.

Ditisheim, M. "Le travail de l'histoire de vie comme instrument de formation en éducation" (The use of the life history as an instrument of development in education). *Education Permanente*, 1984, *72–73*, 199–210.

Dominicé, P. *La formation enjeu de l'évaluation* (Adult learning and development as key question to the practice of evaluation). Berne: Peter Kang, 1979.

Dominicé, P. *L'histoire de vie comme processus de formation* (Life history as a process of development). Paris: L'Harmattan, 1990.

Dominicé, P. "Les formateurs d'adultes doivent-ils obtenir une certification pour être autorisés à pratiquer l'histoire de vie en formation?" (Must adult educators be certified in order to practice the life history approach in adult education?). In P. Alehit, A. Bron-Wojciechowska, E. Brugger, and P. Dominicé (eds.), *The Biographical Approach in European Adult Education*. Vienna: Verband Wiener Volksbildung, 1995.

Dominicé, P. "Faire une place à la formation dans le champ des sciences humaines, ou la biographie éducative à la lumière de ses origines" *Pratiques de Formation* (University of Paris), 1996, 8(31), 93–102.

Dominicé, P., and others. *Les origines biographiques de la compétence d'apprendre* (The biographical origins of learning ability). Cahiers de la Section des Sciences de l'Education, no. 87. Geneva: Université de Genève, 1999.

Egger, R. "Hidden Stories: Biographical Research in Its Social and Ethical Context." In P. Alheit, A. Bron-Wojciechowska, E. Brugger, and P. Dominicé (eds.), *The Biographical Approach in European Adult Education*. Vienna: Verband Wiener Volksbildung, 1995.

Erikson, E. *Childhood and Society*. New York: Norton, 1963.

Erikson, E. *Adulthood: Essays*. New York: Norton, 1978.

F. Tyler Daiels Co. *University Library of Autobiography*. 15 vols. New York: F. Tyler Daiels, 1918.

Ferrarotti, F. *Histoire et histoire de vie* (History and life history). Paris: Méridiens, 1983.

Finger, M. *Biographie et herméneutique: Les aspects épistémologiques et méthodologiques de la méthode biographique* (Biography and hermeneutics: Epistemological and methodological aspects of the biographical method). Montreal: Université de Montréal, Faculté d'Education Permanente, 1984.

Finger, M. *Apprendre une issue: L'éducation des adultes à l'âge de la transformation de perspective* (Learning an issue: Adult education in an age of perspective transformation). Lausanne: Editions LEP (Loisirs et Pédagogie), 1989.

Freire, P. *Pedagogy of the Oppressed*. New York: Seabury Press, 1970.

Gaulejac, V. de. *La nevrose de classe* (Class neurosis). Paris: Hommes et Groupes, 1987.

Gaulejac, V. de, and Taboada Léonetti, I. *La Lutte des places* (The battle for a place). Paris: Desclée de Brouwer, 1994.

Gilligan, C. *In a Different Voice*. Cambridge, Mass.: Harvard University Press, 1982.

Glaser, B. G., and Strauss, A. L. *The Discovery of Grounded Theory: Strategies for Qualitative Research*. New York: Aldine de Gruyter, 1967.

Gould, R. *Transformations, Growth and Change in Adult Life*. New York: Simon & Schuster, 1978.

Hatch, J. A., and Wisniewski, R. (eds.). *Life History and Narrative*. Bristol, Pa.: Falmer Press, 1995.

Havighurst, R. J. *Human Development and Education*. White Plains, N.Y.: Longman, 1953.

Houde, R. *Les temps de la vie* (Times of life). Chicoutimi, Quebec: Gaetan Morin, 1986.

Houle, C. O. *Continuing Learning in the Professions*. San Francisco: Jossey-Bass, 1980.

Huberman, A. M. *La vie des enseignants* (The life cycle of teachers). Neuchâtel: Delachaux et Niestlé, 1990.

Jackson, L., and Caffarella, R. S. (eds.). *Experiential Learning: A New Approach*. New Directions for Adult and Continuing Education, no. 67. San Francisco: Jossey-Bass, 1994.

Jarvis, P. *Adult Learning in the Social Context*. London: Croon Helm, 1987.

Jennett, P. A., and Pearson, T. G. "Educational Responses to Practice-Based Learning: Recent Innovations in Medicine." In H. K. Baskett and V. J. Marsick (eds.), *Professionals' Ways of Knowing: New Findings on How to Improve Professional Education*. New Directions for Adult and Continuing Education, no. 55. San Francisco: Jossey-Bass, 1992.

Johnson-Bailey, J., and Cervero, R. M. "An Analysis of the Educational Narratives of Reentry Black Women." *Adult Education Quarterly*, 1996, 46(3), 142–157.

Josso, C. *Cheminer vers soi* (Approaching oneself). Lausanne: L'Age d'Homme, 1991.

Josso, C., Bausch, H., Dominicé, P., and Finger, M. *Les formateurs d'adulte et leur formation* (Adult educators and their education). Cahiers de la Section des Sciences de l'Education, no. 58. Geneva: Université de Genève, 1990.

Kaufman, S. R. *The Ageless Self: Sources of Meaning in Late Life*. New York: New American Library, 1968.

Keen, S., and Valley-Fox, A. *Your Mythic Journey: Finding Meaning in Your Life Through Writing and Storytelling*. New York: Putnam, 1989.

Kegan, R. *In over Our Heads: The Mental Demands of Modern Life*. Cambridge, Mass.: Harvard University Press, 1996.

Kimmel, D. C. *Adulthood and Aging: An Interdisciplinary, Developmental View*. New York: Wiley, 1980.

Knowles, M. S. *The Modern Practice of Adult Education: Andragogy Versus Pedagogy*. New York: Association Press, 1973.

Knowles, M. S. *The Adult Learner: A Neglected Species*. (3rd ed.) Houston, Tex.: Gulf, 1984.

Knox, A. B. *Adult Development and Learning: A Handbook on Individual Growth and Competence in the Adult Years*. San Francisco: Jossey-Bass, 1977.

Kohli, M. "The World We Forgot: An Historical Review of the Life Course." In V. W. Marshall (ed.), *Later Life: The Social Psychology of Aging*. Thousand Oaks, Calif.: Sage, 1986.

Kuhlen, R. G. *Psychological Backgrounds of Adult Education*. Notes and Essays on Education for Adults, no. 40. Syracuse: Center for the Study of Liberal Education for Adults, 1970.

Kübler-Ross, E. *Les derniers instants de la vie* (On death and dying). Geneva: Labor et Fides, 1969.

Lalive d'Epinay, C. *Entre retraite et vieillesse: Travaux de sociologie compréhensive*. Lausanne: Editions Réalités Sociales, 1996.

Lasker, H. M., and Moore, J. F. "Current Studies of Adult Development: Implications for Education." Unpublished manuscript, Cambridge, Mass., 1979.

Legrand, M. *L'approche biographique* (The biographical approach). Paris: Hommes et Perspectives, EPI, 1993.

Lejeune, P. *L'autobiographie en France* (Autobiography in France). Paris: Armand Colin, 1971.

Lejeune, P. *Je est un autre: L'autobiographie, de la littérature aux médias* (I is another: The autobiography from literature to media). Paris: Editions du Seuil, 1980.

Levinson, D. *The Seasons of a Man's Life*. New York: Ballantine, 1978.

Lewis, O. *The Children of Sanchez: Autobiography of a Mexican Family*. New York: Vintage Books, 1961.

Loevinger, J. *Ego Development: Conceptions and Theories*. San Francisco: Jossey-Bass, 1976.

Mader, W. (ed.). *Adult Education in the Federal Republic of Germany: Scholarly Approaches and Professional Practice*. Vancouver: University of British Columbia, 1992.

Merriam, S. *Adult Development: Implications for Adult Education*. ERIC Clearinghouse on Adult, Career and Vocational Education, Information Series, no. 282. Columbus, Ohio: National Center for Research in Vocational Education, 1984.

Merriam, S. (ed.). *An Update on Adult Learning Theory*. New Directions for Adult and Continuing Education, no. 57. San Francisco: Jossey-Bass, 1993.

Merriam, S. B., and Brockett, R. *The Profession and Practice of Adult Education*. San Francisco: Jossey-Bass, 1997.

Mezirow, J. *Transformative Dimensions of Adult Learning*. San Francisco: Jossey-Bass, 1991.

Mezirow, J., and Associates. *Fostering Critical Reflection in Adulthood: A Guide to Transformative and Emancipatory Learning.* San Francisco: Jossey-Bass, 1990.

Miller, A. *For Your Own Good: Hidden Cruelty in Child-Rearing and the Roots of Violence* (Hildegarde and Hunter Hannum, trans.). New York: Farrar, Straus, Giroux, 1983.

Misch, G. *Geschichte des Autobiographie* (History of autobiography), Vol. 7. Berlin: Teubner, 1907.

Neugarten, B. L. *Personality in Middle and Late Life.* Rockaway Beach, N.Y.: Lieber-Atherton, 1964.

Neuhauser, P. C. *Corporate Legends and Lore.* New York: McGraw- Hill, 1993.

Oliveira, R. D. de. *Le Féminin Ambigu* (The Ambiguous feminine). Geneva: Concept Moderne, 1989.

Peck, T. A. "Women's Self-Definition in Adulthood." *Psychology of Women Quarterly,* 1986, *10,* 274–284.

Pineau, G. *Vies des histoires de vie* (The history of life history). Montreal: Université de Montréal, Faculté d'Education Permanente, 1980.

Pineau, G., and Legrand, J.-L. *Les Histoires de Vie* (Histories of life). Paris: Les Presses Universitaires de France, 1993.

Pineau, G., and Marie-Michèle. *Produire sa vie: Autoformation et autobiographie* (Creating one's life: Self-development and autobiography). Montreal: Editions Saint-Martin, 1983.

Pratt, D. D. "Andragogy as a Relational Construct." *Adult Education Quarterly,* 1988, *38*(3), 160–172.

Ricoeur, P. *Du texte à l'action: Essai d'herméneutique.* (From text to action: Essay in hermeneutics). Vol. 2. Paris: Editions du Seuil, 1986.

Riverin-Simard, D. *Etapes de vie au travail* (Stages of life at work). Montreal: Editions Saint-Martin, 1984.

Riverin-Simard, D. *Transitions professionnelles* (Vocational transitions). Sainte-Foy: Les Presses de l'Université Laval, 1993.

Robin, G. *Guide en reconnaissance des acquis* (Guide for credit unit validation, 5th ed.). Montreal: Editions Vermette, 1992.

Rogers, C. *Freedom to Learn.* Columbus, Ohio: Merrill, 1969.

Rossiter, M., and Weingand, D. E. *Life Stories in Library Programming.* Madison: University of Wisconsin, 1996.

Schön, D. A. *Educating the Reflective Practitioner.* San Francisco: Jossey-Bass, 1987.

Schwartz, B. *L'éducation demain* (Tomorrow's education). Paris: Aubier Montaigne, 1973.

Smith, R. M., and Associates. *Learning to Learn Across the Life Span.* San Francisco: Jossey-Bass, 1990.

Staude, J. R. *The Adult Development of C. G. Jung.* New York: Routledge, 1981.

Tennant, M., and Pogson, P. *Learning and Change in the Adult Years: A Developmental Perspective.* San Francisco: Jossey-Bass, 1995.

Theiss, W. *The "Siberian Children": A History of the Polish Children Repatriated from Siberia and Manchuria in the Years 1919–1923*. Warsaw: University of Warsaw, 1991.

Thomas, W., and Znaniecke, F. *The Polish Peasant in Europe and America: Monograph of an Immigrant Group*. 2 vols. New York: Octagon, 1974. (Originally published 1918.)

Touraine, A. *Critique de la modernité* (Critique of modernity). Paris: Fayard, 1992.

Vermersch, P. *L'entretien d'explicitation* (The interview of explanation). Paris: ESF Editeur, 1994.

West, L. *Beyond Fragments: Adults, Motivation and Higher Education*. Basingstoke, UK: Taylor and Francis, 1996.

Index